Gathered at Albany

by

Allan J. Janssen

The Historical Series of the Reformed Church in America
No. 25

Gathered at Albany

A History of a Classis

by

Allan J. Janssen

WILLIAM B. EERDMANS PUBLISHING COMPANY
GRAND RAPIDS, MICHIGAN

© 1995 Wm. B. Eerdmans Publishing Co.
255 Jefferson Ave. S.E., Grand Rapids, MI 49503

Printed in the United States of America

ISBN 0-8028-0594-9

Contents

The Historical Series of the Reformed Church in America

This series has been inaugurated by the General Synod of the Reformed Church in America acting through its Commission on History for the purpose of encouraging historical research and providing a medium wherein this knowledge may be shared with the academic community and with members of the denomination in order that a knowledge of the past may contribute to right action in the present.

General Editor

The Rev. Donald J. Bruggink, Ph.D.
Western Theological Seminary

Acknowledgements

My father was a preacher. He was also the stated clerk of his classis. He would have us children lined up in that midwestern parsonage living room, dealing out pages of classis minutes like undersized riverboat gamblers. "Classis" was a mysterious, but certainly important part of church life. That was evident as we overheard Dad talk over classis business with his colleagues. To be a church was to be related to this indistinct entity, near yet far. In the turn of generations, I found myself occupying the role of stated clerk of a classis far distant from the Dakota prairie, in Albany. The distance was more than geographical, for Albany had a classis from the beginning of the Reformed church's separate existence on this continent. Still, the classis retained a place of honor and, indeed, of power. What makes a classis? This history owes its inception to that Dakota upbringing, now transferred to the capital of New York State.

Since no study can claim to be the result of individual effort and initiative, I owe a debt to a variety of persons and institutions. Of special mention is the committee of the Albert A. Smith Fellowship who honored me with one of their awards that provided time and resources to mine the Reformed church archives at New Brunswick, New Jersey. John Coakley encouraged me through thoughtful suggestion and support. Russell Gasero, the Reformed church archivist, was untiring in providing me with records from the church's past. Three other institutions offered me great support, perhaps without their conscious knowledge. St. Anthony-on-the-Hudson, a Franciscan retreat center with a theological library, provided me space (and a microfilm reader!) where much of the research and writing could take place. I thank especially Brother Jim Doyle for his kind cooperation. The church I serve, the First Reformed Church of Bethlehem, continues to support what we used to call a "learned ministry," encouraging its pastor in pursuits that seem far distant from the current rage for "functional ministry." And of course, I am obligated to my colleagues in the Classis of Albany. In living with the classis through two centuries plus, I found myself to be a colleague of all the saints and scoundrels (often both in the same person!) who have prayed and worshiped and debated and rejoiced together throughout what has become a "history." Finally, I must acknowledge great debt to my children, Jonathan, Sarah, and Emily, and my wife, Colleen, who not only continue to encourage me, but put up with me in my absences, in my frustrations, and even in my excitements when I would gleefully announce a bit of classis news from generations past!

Allan Janssen
Easter, 1994

Foreword

This is an important study in local Reformed church history and a worthy volume in the "Historical Series." The study is important for several reasons. First, it is a superbly researched local history: it tells the story of a *classis* in the Reformed Church in America, the Classis of Albany, New York, from its beginning in 1771 to 1979. Allan Janssen successfully keeps the churches *Gathered at Albany* at center stage throughout the book.

That is a surprising accomplishment. Virtually every study of this genre I know about is either an "historical directory" on the one hand, or a history of selected congregations within the classis on the other. This book is significantly different. Janssen helps us see that a classis is more than the sum of its parts and is a unique and living organism with a particular history in its own right. That is what he carefully examines in this study. As such his book offers a creative and promising new model for local Reformed church historiography.

Second, the book is a persuasive apologetic for the role of the classis in Reformed polity. Janssen knows the *Book of Church Order*, which positions the classis as a "mediating institution" between the local churches and the General Synod: "The local churches exist neither autonomously...nor as an expression of the General Synod, but in an intercongregational reality called classis." In that position, the classis exists to ensure and protect the integrity, faith, and practice of its member churches and clergy.

The major story threading its way through this book tells how the Classis of Albany sustained that role in the face of numerous

ix

delicate and difficult pressures "from below" and "from above."
Among the more serious of these were questions on theology,
ecumenicity, polity, social justice, church and state, and especially
women's ordination, a cause celebre in the classis and church in
the late 1970s to which Janssen devotes an entire chapter. In
telling this story, Janssen shows that a classis can on occasion take
bold and daring initiatives to effect change in both church and
society. He also shows that churches can debate controversial and
even scandalous questions without destroying people or tearing
apart the institution. For that reason alone, the book is both
timely and instructive.

Third, this study is important because its subject is the Albany
Classis, arguably the most historically significant local judicatory
in the Reformed Church in America. Strategically situated at the
center of traffic between the "liberal" New England theology to
the east and the democratizing influence of the expanding
frontier to the west, the Albany churches during the eighteenth
and nineteenth centuries were the first among the (Dutch)
Reformed on this continent to interact with an unfamiliar New
World context and be challenged on substantive and long held
positions of faith and practice.

Janssen carefully analyzed this interaction and tells why the
churches *Gathered at Albany* sometimes learned to sing a new
rendition of "the Lord's song" in this "strange land." In
subsequent years, until at least the end of the nineteenth century,
as the (Dutch) Reformed church spread here and there
throughout the expanding nation and faced similar challenges,
the Albany experience often served the denomination as a helpful
and influential model. In all of this, Janssen tells a fascinating
story: the story of the Americanization of an Old World classis.

Gathered at Albany is a notable achievement in Reformed
historiography. And for good reason. Allan Janssen has spent
nearly his entire professional career as pastor-scholar-leader
within the Albany Classis. He is a voracious reader, a productive
and dedicated churchman, and a recognized and creative student
of Calvin and the Reformed tradition; when I was his colleague in
Albany during the 1980s, I often referred to him as "our Jonathan
Edwards," and I meant that as a serious characterization.

This book is a solid study in local Reformed church history

and, among other things, makes a profound statement on the role of the classis in Reformed polity. But it is also more than that. The study provides a window through which the reader can view some of the great questions and challenges Reformed Christians gathered in any time or place must continue to face if they would be faithful to the Lord of the Church.

James W. Van Hoeven
First Presbyterian Church
Hastings, Nebraska
Advent, 1994

Introduction

The story of Albany's churches begins in 1642, the earliest days of the city's settlement by European colonists, when the Dutch colonists brought their brand of Christianity, now called "Reformed," to what was then Fort Orange.[1] More than a century later, the Dutch churches in and around Albany were to begin to form themselves into a classis. This book describes the history of the Classis of Albany.

Because this is a history of a classis, it will be an investigation of a particular sort, a species of local history. Local church histories generally are written in celebration of a milestone anniversary of a congregation and are of widely varying historical quality, but they indicate an important theological reality. Despite the fact that much church history is written as history of "the" Christian church, or of a particular expression that claims to be "the" church, it is in the local church that God meets God's people in word and sacrament. The Spirit gathers and shapes people into communities of faith—particular, ordinary bodies. Their histories tell their stories, and their stories can express a particularity absent in broader church histories.

A history of a classis differs from most local histories in that it is not the history of a particular congregation but of a number of churches gathered into a larger body. It is tempting to see the classis only as an aggregate of its churches, and to examine its history by telling the stories of the individual churches within its bounds—a particular, relatively compact geographical area. In fact, most classis histories do precisely that, and thus are little more than historical directories.[2] This study, however, treats the classis as a distinct body which expresses its life in a particular way.

1

What happened when the clergy and elders gathered? What issues troubled them? What directions did their life together take? What happened in this institution? The various classes were to express a particular way of being church. For the Reformed, a church did not exist as a separate congregation. But neither did the congregation exist as an instantiation of a national or global institution. A church exists as it is gathered into a public community. Or, as the Heidelberg Catechism puts it: "...the Son of God, by his Spirit and his Word, gathers, protects, and preserves for himself, in the unity of the true faith, a congregation..." (Ans, 54). This is true of the local congregation gathered in worship, of course, but it is also true of the consistory gathered in leadership. But more so, the congregation existed within a classis.

The various classes were to express a particular way of being church. The notion and fact of a "classis" surfaced in 1571 at the Synod of Emden, in East Friesland. This synod in "exile" of the Netherlands church decreed that a "classical convention," composed of a few churches contiguous to each other, be held once every three to six months. Furthermore, the synod formed six classes in Germany and the southern part of the Netherlands.[3]

The classis functions as a "mediating institution," a public arena in which local congregations meet to be the church in a transparochial setting. It remains local, in that it is geographically concentrated and its concerns reflect its locality. It thus expresses the Reformed idea of church as a public institution, albeit with a local flavor. Local churches exist, in Reformed thinking, neither autonomously nor primarily as expressions of the General Synod, but in a local, public, intercongregational reality called classis.

The classis as an institution presented an odd way of being church in the America coming of age, standing as it does against a deep current of radical democracy or populism in American thought. As nineteenth-century historian Alexis De Tocqueville noted in a chapter of Democracy in America entitled "The Influence of Democracy upon Religion":

It must be acknowledged that equality, which brings great

benefits into the world, nevertheless suggests to men...some very dangerous propensities. It tends to isolate them from each other, to concentrate every man's attention upon himself; and it lays open the soul to an inordinate love of material gratification.[4]

The Classis of Albany came into existence and found its life within the tension De Tocqueville describes. Nathan Hatch, another nineteenth-century author, claims that "religious populism, reflecting the passions of ordinary people and the charisma of democratic movement builders, remains among the oldest and deepest impulses in American life." [5]

In its classes, the Reformed church came up against such populist, or, if you will, democratic impulses in American religious life. It will become clear that the classis most certainly reflected the growing reality of American individualism. Nevertheless, simply by existing, the classis resisted the full impact of individualism. For example, a man (and it was only men through most of this history) could not get himself ordained simply because he felt himself called of God, nor even if his local church confirmed the call. It was to be the task of a gathered people who spent considerable time, energy, and money interviewing, training, and examining the candidate before the classis ordained him to ministry.

The significance of the role of the classis in this example can be seen in the distress of an anonymous contributor to the *Lutheran* magazine, a publication from central New York State Lutherans. The author complained about the appearance of "impostors," men who set themselves up as Lutheran ministers and thereby wreaked havoc in local congregations. It seems that it was incumbent upon the local church to protect itself from rogue preachers. The anonymous author writes:

When they [the congregation] wish to procure a Minister, the question is not, Is he properly qualified?—Is he a man possessing sound knowledge and approved piety?—Has he been regularly licensed or ordained by the constituted authorities of the Church? Is he recommended by an ecclesiastical body in which we can place confidence? But the enquiry usually made on such occasions, and which often determines the location of a Minster, is;—Is he cheap?—Will he labor for such a compensation as we are willing to give him? This is the great difficulty in many of our Congregations. And this is the reason why so many of our people are imposed upon, by those treacherous and false-hearted hypocrites, who go about the country, pretending, under the regular sanction of ecclesiastical authority, to preach the Gospel for nothing.[6]

Reformed congregations were to have similar difficulties judging the credentials of their ministers. However, a congregation could never be left on its own. In fact, there was always a higher ecclesiastical authority, even if that authority was none other than fellow ministers and elders from other churches in the county.

The Reformed, then, lived a practical ecclesiology. There is ample evidence that these Reformed elders and dominies shared an almost passionate concern for church order. They were ever tinkering with it, appealing to it, arguing from its premises. There is little evidence, on the other hand, that they reflected theologically on their order. Their ecclesiology was not explicit. At least there is no statement regarding classes like this one in the Liturgy of the Reformed church concerning the consistory:

> The three offices of elder, deacon, and minister of the Word, being joined together in the consistory, thus continue within the Church the unity of these offices in Christ, as so many branches flourishing in the same Vine. In this manner, all things in the Church will be done decently and in order, when faithful men are chosen according to the rule prescribed in the Word of God.[7]

This approach to local church history suffers certain limitations. As already noted, it will not be a history of the congregations within the classis, except as the story of an individual congregation becomes a part of the story of the classis as a body. Neither will it be a religious history of the area encompassed by the classis, again except as that larger history proves necessary to the story.[8] Nor will this be an intellectual history of the classis, although such an approach, could it be done, would be fascinating.

Instead, this study will follow the institution as it functioned and changed in the developing life of a new nation. One way of reading this history is as an observation of the growth and development of Reformed polity, especially at the level of the classis. As such, it supplements Daniel Meeter's fine work on the Constitution of the Reformed Church in America.[9] It so happens that the classis began to take on life at about the same time as the American Revolution was building up its head of steam. The observer can watch this European church as it encounters the American experience. What happens to the church as the American experience filters through the classis? And what happens to the American experience of the churches as they engage the different approach to reality represented by the classis?

Albany's classis offers a convenient perspective from which to watch this development. In fact, it provides a good screen on which to watch the development of the Reformed church itself. Albany was one of the original five classes, and to a large extent has remained intact through the end of the twentieth century. Thus, it has been affected by, and has affected, much of the life and development of the Reformed church as a denomination.

Furthermore, it stands just outside the center of activity regarding major denominational controversies. For example, the nineteenth-century theological debate on the dangers of "Mercersburg theology" happened largely to the south of Albany. Indeed, until well into the twentieth century, when the stormy debates of East and West, liberal and conservative, blew through the denomination, Albany stood moderately away from the vortex, although by the 1960s Albany would take a more radical approach to societal issues. Indeed, in the early days, Albany's geography placed the classis nearer the frontier and its concerns. This may not make for as exciting a set of events as a historian might desire. But it does provide a sideline seat from which to watch the Reformed church evolve from a European to a fully American denomination.

Our story will begin, its *terminus ad quo*, in 1771, with the general acceptance of the Plan of Union. It might be argued that the classis did not begin until 1800 under a reorganization by the newly incorporated General Synod. But that something like a classis was in formation, and that the term was certainly used in the interim, is not in doubt.

I bring the story to a close, its terminus ad quem, in 1978 for two reasons. First, the Synod of Albany realigned its classes in 1978 to add to the Classis of Albany several large congregations from the Classis of Saratoga. The most recent reorganization of classical boundaries of any significance had happened in 1825, when Schenectady became an autonomous classis. The dynamics shifted sufficiently in 1978 to allow me to end the story there with the sense that the story has been brought into the present.

Second, it was in 1978 that the classis voted to ordain Joyce Borgman de Velder, thus beginning a judicial adventure that culminated in a "change" in Reformed church order that allowed for the ordination of women to the ministry of the Word. I conclude this history with that story, not only because it is significant in its own right, but because it illustrates, to a large extent, what the classis had been about during more than two centuries. This "new" decision simply expressed an old way of doing business.

What have I discovered in the two centuries plus that stretch from the days of Livingstone to the present? Several conclusions will be justified. First, the classis of the late eighteenth century would look very familiar to delegates to a classis in the 1990s. The classis then, as now, worried about the state of its ministers and its churches; it created churches and ordained pastors; it kept its watchful eye on church discipline; it mediated the life of the national church experience to the local and the local to the national. It was, and is, a public forum in which the gathered churches propose, debate, and adjudicate, always with an eye on the purpose of the church—however that may be variously interpreted. In very important respects, the classis has not changed fundamentally.

Second, the classis became an American church. It largely accepted the vocabulary of a revivalist America. It became, almost enthusiastically, a part of that American religious invention, the denomination. It shared the culture around itself, seeing itself as part and parcel of the "Protestant empire." It did all this, however, in its own way, filtering everything through the clumsy, time-consuming organism of the gathered church. It accepted American evangelicalism, but on its own terms. Its very organization expressed conservatism, if only because a body like a classis simply cannot change quickly. Thus it often enjoyed the privilege of second thought.

Third, its odd way of being church made for certain difficulties. The Reformed were not positioned to make a quick strike into the frontier. This may have been partly for theological reasons. The Reformed could not accept the Arminian premises of American revivalism. It also may have been, as often asserted, because the Reformed couldn't get ministers ordained fast enough, what with the church's inconvenient requirement of theological training for its pastors. But it may just as well have been because a classis simply could not move quickly. Everything had to be done "by committee." The body met regularly only twice a year, although it met in special session often enough. Even then, physical obstacles like storm or illness often made its work difficult. The odd way of the classis can hardly be claimed to be the most efficient way.

But, fourth, this odd way had strengths as well. It was able to support congregations that otherwise might have perished in the weakness of the moment. It could provide some measure of protection for the congregations as it offered a discipline before which its pastors and consistories were responsible. It provided a "home" for congregations and pastors, not in a distant bishop or denominational offices, but as a local congregation in communion with other congregations. The classis was a place to be church beyond the congregation, face to face, often with people well known to each other.

Fifth, the classis displays a way of being the church that is older than the denomination (as defined in chapter 4). Even in the late twentieth century, following a frenetic period of denominational restructure on top of reorganization, the classes continue to function. They remain the central assembly in Reformed church order.

This is the story of one such assembly.

I
A New Beginning in a New Nation (1771-1820)

In 1820, the Classis of Albany tried the Rev Dr. John Bradford, pastor of the Reformed church in Albany, on charges of public inebriation. Bradford was not only pastor of the classis's premier church, but a man of some reputation in the new nation's ecclesiastical circles. Charles Corwin, citing Sprague's *Annals of the American Pulpit*, notes him to be "reckoned among the distinguished pulpit orators of the day."[1] This sad affair involved the classis in a complicated procedure that included more than a dozen witnesses, and required the classis to sort through the thicket of both discipline and polity, even as the case worked its way to the General Synod. But by 1820, the classis had begun to find its footing as an institution that could withstand the rigors of a major disciplinary tremor with the pastor of its central congregation.

Indeed, the classis by then had grown into a body which could exercise considerable power over both the life of its churches and of its ministers, feeling its way through discipline with a persuasive, rather than coercive, authority. It acted similarly when it came to the admission of ministers. It could not, for example, assign candidates from New Brunswick to pulpits. But it could, theoretically, keep certain "foreign" influences out. And it would try.

Beginnings

Within fifty years, then, the classis had grown from nonexistence to a position of significant power in the life of the

Reformed church. How did this growth occur? In large measure, it was through a church order that gave considerable power to the classis. Nevertheless, the American democratic experiment was to work its modulating effect on a European church order transplanted to American shores.

Evidence that the Albany Classis was alive and at work at the end of the eighteenth century is sketchy. Minutes of the classis for this period are not available. All evidence is second-hand: from the minutes of the General Synod or from the Particular Synod. Even in these shadows, however, one can observe the classis beginning to function as a new institution, feeling its way. Already, it had begun to function as a mediating structure—between the churches of the classis and between the local church now embodied in a classis and the national church as expressed in the General Synod—and finding its way on a new path in a (relatively) new land.

The story of the Classis of Albany begins with the resolution of the struggle for the independence of the American Dutch church from the Classis of Amsterdam. It is not necessary to recount the full narrative of the well-known "Coetus-Conferentie" dispute. The substance of that controversy is, however, germane. At issue was the power of the *classis*. The colonial churches subsisted within the care of the Classis of Amsterdam, and it was the power of that classis to examine and to ordain ministers that provoked the American churches to push for some sort of independence. Not that the Americans disputed the power of a classis to ordain. They simply desired a means by which the power could be sifted through the new American experience. The American churches needed ministers, and in their circumstance could not wait for candidates to make the trip to the Netherlands for an extended period of study. The churches on this side of the ocean needed something like a classis in order to function at all like a church.[2]

The Coetus-Conferentie schism lost its power in October of 1771, when the ministers and elders of the various Reformed Dutch churches in the colonies met in New York to adopt a Plan of Union. Struck as a compromise, largely through the genius of John Livingstone, the plan set forth an organization within the outlines of the church order formulated by the Synod of Dort. That international Reformed synod is perhaps best known for the canons enshrined in the confessional standards of the Reformed church. However, its church order has most likely had the more lasting influence, as this study will seek to show.

The Plan of Union established two bodies: general assemblies and particular assemblies. It refused to designate these bodies as synods and classes, most likely in sensitivity to the recent disputes over the various powers of classis and coetus. While Dort outlined four ecclesiastical assemblies—general (or national) synod, particular synod, classis, and consistory—the plan omitted the particular synod and assumed the presence of the consistory.

The plan designated five particular assemblies: New York, New Brunswick, Hackensack, Kingston, and Albany. The particular assembly of Albany was to be held alternately in Albany and Schenectady, and it included the churches in the counties of Albany, Gloucester, and Cumberland, most of present New York state above Kingston.[3]

The particular assemblies possessed limited powers. Dort's church order had described the various assemblies as "greater" and "lesser." The greater assembly was to attend to matters beyond the capability of the lesser or to such matters that pertain to all the congregations that compose the greater body. Similarly, the Plan of Union described what was to be considered in the particular assembly:

all matters regarding the interests of subordinate congregations, and which cannot be determined by the consistories, shall in the first instance, be regularly brought forward, and acted upon, (even to the suspension of ministers for improper conduct,) before they can be brought up to a higher tribunal.[4]

The particular assembly acted, then, as a sort of intermediary institution—somewhere between the congregation and the General Assembly. Matters could, and often were, brought to the General Assembly for ajudication. It is to be noted, however, that the particular assembly did not hold the power to form churches, or to ordain ministers.

Indeed, little seemed to be expected of the particular assemblies. They were expressly instructed not to hold more than one ordinary meeting a year, "on account of the distance of the respective members from each other."[5]

Most importantly, the General Assembly reserved for itself the power to examine students for ministry, both for acceptance as candidates and for licensure and ordination. The difficulty in wresting control over students for ministry from the Classis of Amsterdam is reflected here, and the General Assembly was not about to cede its power to the "lesser" bodies. There is little evidence of the presence and work of the particular assembly of Albany in the earliest years. The minutes of the General Meeting of Ministers and Elders in October, 1773, record as present: "From the Particular Body of Albany.—Drs. Joannes Casp. Freyenmont and Joannes Scheunema, Ministers at Kinderhook, &c. and Catskill &c., with Messrs. Henricus Oothout and Jacobus Viele, Elders at Catskill and Scaghticoke."[6] Albany did not, however, send delegates again until 1783 (although the General Assembly itself was interrupted by war from 1775-1778). The General Assembly remarked in 1778 that the Albany body had for a considerable time been "disturbed by intestine foes and the barbarous Indians, as instigated by the enemy" and therefore had been unable to meet.[7]

Still, in 1780 the General Assembly was sufficiently concerned to write Albany to ask why their delegates had not yet shown. The concern escalated the following year, prompting an "earnest exhortation...not to neglect attendance at the ecclesiastical meetings, but anew to resume it to the honor of God and the welfare of his Church." Since Albany didn't show up in 1782 and had not in fact responded to the letter sent the previous year, the assembly expressed "heartfelt grief," since Albany's absence resulted in "great injury which the Church of God suffers from these failures and neglects...."[8] The following year, without recorded explanation, the delegates from Albany appeared.

In 1784, the General Assembly listed the make-up of the particular bodies. The list of Albany churches and ministers read:

Albany	Eilardus Westerlo, outstanding
" German Congregation	Vacant
Schenectady	Berend Vroman, emeritus
Conewango	Thomas Romeyn
Normanskill	"
Upper and Lower Schoharie	"
Stone Arabia	"

Canajoharie	"
Great Flats	Rosekrans
Catskill and	
Coxsackie	Joannes Shunoma
Manor Livingston,	
Greenbush and	
Taghkanick	Nicholas Lansingh
Claverack	Gebhart
Kinderhook	Vacant
Schodack	"
Half Moon	"
Saratoga	"
Schaghticoke	Elias Van Bunschoten[9]

It was not the case, however, that all the churches had become a part of the particular body (which had been called a classis since 1784). Indeed, the flagship church of the classis, the church in Albany, did not subscribe to the Plan of Union. While the pastors of that church had consistently promoted the plan, the consistory remained aloof, much as they had remained neutral in the warfare between the coetus and the conferentie. Nor was Albany alone; several churches followed its example. It wasn't until October, 1785, that the General Synod[10] noted that the classis reported that the "Dutch congregation at Albany has subscribed to the Articles of Union, and have been received as a member of that Rev. Classis."[11]

There is, however, evidence of the classis at work in the care of ministers and churches. The General Assembly reported in 1780 that Nicolas Lansingh presented himself to the classis for examination for ministry. He brought with him credentials from, among others, Eilardus Westerlo, "under whose direction he pursued studies in Sacred Theology."[12]

In 1786, the classis had attempted to discover by what authority a certain G. W. Snyder was acting as a minister in Schoharie. The General Synod entrusted the investigation of the matter to the classis. The synod had it "on report" that Snyder, following a request of the synod to delay his examination, had been ordained by the Coetus of Pennsylvania. The synod suggested that the classis might have to approach that (German) body. Following some inquiry, Eilardus Westerlo reported to the synod that the consistory at Schoharie had written "various offensive remarks" about the classis and the synod and threatened to withdraw. The General Synod then determined to open correspondance with the coetus with a "kind, fraternal letter."[13]

Several issues that would confront the classis over the next century surfaced in the affair of the Rev. Winslow Paige in 1792. Paige was a Congregational minister examined and received into the classis. Paige was then given a position in the Schagticoke congregation. That congregation already had a minister, Lambertus De Ronde, who introduced a charge against Paige. De Ronde wrote the General Synod detailing services led by Paige in the Schagticoke church not approved by the consistory and illegal according to the classis. The synod referred to Article XV of the Constitution (Dort) which stated that no minister was to preach indiscriminately in a place without the authority of a synod or classis, nor was he to preach nor to administer sacraments in a church not his own without the consent of the consistory of the church where he intended to minister.[14] Here, then, we see discipline at work, the troubling question of the relation of the Dutch church to other churches raised, concern over the introduction of ministers outside the Dutch church aired, and the care of congregations exercised.

Another issue facing the young Classis of Albany concerned the visitation of the churches under its care. Such visitation was prescribed by the church order of Dort, which instructed the classis, in the person of its two oldest and most experienced pastors, to visit each congregation once a year. This order was to confound the classis (and the General Synod) for years to come. Already in 1784, the synod had imposed the duty on the classes to visit the churches under their care. The Albany Classis reported to the 1785 meeting of the synod that it had the matter on the books but had yet to do anything about it. In October, 1786, the classis could report that it had directed its visitors to perform the task at the "earliest possible time."[15]

A major change in the life of the Dutch Reformed church occurred in 1792 with the appearance of the Explanatory Articles of the Government and Discipline. The articles were meant to adapt Dort's order to the American context. In fact, it was to give the American church something like its own constitution. In the process, the new articles devolved greater power to the classes.

In practical terms, this meant that the classes could now ordain ministers of the Word. Indeed, in 1797, the Classis of Albany ordained Robert McDowall, who shortly thereafter left for Canada, so initiating the missionary work of the Reformed church. (The story of the work in Canada is told in chapter 2.)

The 1800 General Synod effected a major reorganization. With the Explanatory Articles of 1792, the synod had reinstated the particular synod as an assembly, although as there was only one such synod, it was coextensive with the General Synod. In 1800, the synod created the Particular Synod of Albany and divided the Classis of Albany into three parts: the Classes of Rensselaer, Montgomery and Albany. Albany's classis consisted of:

Albany	Basic [Westerlo]	Salem
Bethlehem	Niskayuna	Helderbergh
Coeymans	Schenectady	Beaver Dam
Coxsackie	Jerusalem	Woestyne and Boght

The synod added this note: "The churches formed in Canada, until they are sufficiently numerous to form a separate Classis, are to be annexed to the Classis of Albany."[16] We see in this list the core of the classis that will remain for the next two centuries (with one major division coming with the separation of the Classis of Schenectady in 1826).

The synod ordered the new Classis of Albany to meet on the last Wednesday of July, 1800, at the Albany church. The Rev. Dr. Dirck Romeyn, of the Schenectady church, was to preach the sermon and to organize the classis. However, when the day and the preacher arrived, confusion reigned. Following the dissolution of the old classis, no one knew exactly what day and time the General Synod had ordered for the formation of the new one. No one had received copies of the minutes of the General Synod; thus it was informally determined that the new classis could not be organized. Romeyn asked to be dismissed to return to Schenectady and promptly left. However, some time later that same afternoon, two members of the new classis showed up and asserted that *they* were fully convinced that this was the day and place and that the classis could legally constitute itself. With that, the brethren convened at the "Old Dutch Church" to form the classis. Listed present were the Revs. John Bassett and John

Johnson of the Albany church with their elder Jacob Pruyne, the
Rev. John Demarest of Niskayuna with his elder Jacob Lansing,
and the Rev. Jacob Sickles of Coxsackie and Coeymans with his
elder Philip Conine. It being "too far advanced in the evening to
have a sermon preached," they opened the classis with a prayer.
They elected John Bassett as it first president and John Johnson
as secretary and treasurer. Thus began the classis afresh.[17]

Becoming a Classis

Following reorganization of the classes, Albany's classis groped
its way into a new era. Its formative years paralleled the nation's
period of democratization as it moved into its republican reality.
As Nathan Hatch puts it, "this vast transformation, this shift away
from the Enlightenment and classical republicanism toward
vulgar democracy and materialistic individualism in a matter of
decades, was the real American Revolution."[18] Albany was to
experience the beginning of this democratic revolution as its
population increased three-fold between 1790 and 1810, most of
the growth coming from New England Yankees.[19] Albany's
churches were not home to enlistees in radical democratic
experimentation. Instead, the churches were to find their way in
ordered relations between themselves and with the classis as an
institution. What shape would this new ecclesiastical order take?

Already in 1801, the relationship between the classis and the
particular synod took on a financial character. The particular synod
had required $110 from the classis. The classis in turn
apportioned the sum among its congregations. The schedule of
payments suggests the relative strengths of the congregations:

Albany	$40
Schenectady	20
Boght	5
Coeymans & Coxsackie	15
Jerusalem, Helderbergh, & Salem	15
Nessikauna	7
Basick	3

Beaver-Dam   5

The classis added that if congregations collected more than their allotment, the classis would gladly receive the money on deposit and "sacredly" set the money aside for mission. In what was to become a habit, the treasurer of the synod reported at the next meeting that only the Albany church had paid![20] It is important to note that the particular synod did not directly assess the churches. Nor for that matter did it use the classis as intermediary, as a sort of collection agent. The classis itself, as an integral institution, was assessed. Of course, the classis existed only as a confederation of its several congregations and could raise the money only by appealing to its various consistories and congregations. Even then it did not, perhaps could not, require payment. It received its money through a voluntary collection from the churches. Still, it was the *classis* that bore the financial responsibility.

But the classis had a more direct responsibility to the churches within its bounds. It was more than a loose collection of congregations. The Explanatory Articles had enjoined the classes to conduct a yearly visitation of the churches. For the "more uniform and proper execution" of this particular duty, the General Synod may agree upon certain questions that will then be included in the records of the classes (Art. 44). This article "explained" the injuction of the church order of Dort we have already encountered that authorized two of the classis's "eldest, most experienced, and best qualified of its members" to visit the churches to inquire as to the practice of the officeholders, sound doctrine and discipline, and the proper edification of the congregation, most especially its youth (Art. 44).

Church visitation quickly became an issue that would trouble the church for decades to come. Already in 1800 the General Synod had proposed a plan for church visitation. The synod's reasons for developing the new plan hint at the state of the practice at that time. The synod noted that the procedure was a greater departure from church order than necessary. What was that procedure? Two of synod's reasons suggest that visitation was happening at the classis meetings themselves. The synod noted that a classis could not expect to receive an accurate representation when it is made by only one member of the consistory. The synod also noted that the new proposal would prevent many "disagreeable disputes and altercations between the members of Classis, at their meetings."

The synod consequently devised a method by which each classis would divide into two or more districts (unless it be small enough in geography for one) and appoint "the most prudent and faithful" minister in each district to visit the congregation. He was to visit each congregation once each year. However, the synod allowed that if a church was too far distant, it could still be visited at the classis meeting.[21]

In 1807, the Albany Classis recommended an alternate proposal to the particular synod that would designate all the ministers of the classis as visitors. Two ministers would visit each church. At the conclusion of the visit, one of the ministers would preach a sermon "adapted as much as possible to the situation and circumstances of the congregation." The particular synod rejected the proposal and commended its classes to comply with the constitution. The particular synod noted the following year that it appeared that the classis had not completed its visitation, but in 1810, the classis reported that it had visited some of the churches and expected to get to them all by the next meeting of the classis.[22]

The classis evidenced its concern for the life of the congregations in a directive to its delegates to particular synod in 1801. The classis desired the synod to devise some way to prevent unnecessary oaths, cursing, swearing, and profanation of the Lord's Day. While this early "social concern" was broader than the internal life of the congregations, a third concern fits very much the concern of the church order of Dort: the preaching of the Heidelberg Catechism. The classis wanted the synod to remedy the neglect of its ministers to preach the catechism.[23] The synod replied that it certainly could do nothing about public cursing and swearing; that was the purview of the Legislature.

However, the synod instructed the presidents of the various classes to make strictest inquiries whether the ministers preach regularly on the catechism, and to warn the members of the churches both publicly and privately on sin and error.[24] The classis in turn instructed its ministers to preach from the catechism, "any consistorial resolves to the contrary notwithstanding."[25] As shall be clear, continued injunctions on catechetical preaching suggest that the catechism was honored more in the breach than in the execution. Indeed, the classis did not force the issue by bringing the weight of discipline against either minister or consistory. However, the classis never questioned its authority to demand that the practice be followed.

At about the same time, the particular synod urged catechetical instruction of the "blacks." Blacks, most likely slaves or servants in the employ of church members, were considered part of the household. The synod noted with satisfaction that most classes, Albany included, had complied with this instruction. Albany's own records, however, report that while some places had instituted catechetical lectures for blacks, it was a sporadic attempt at best. Classis then "earnestly recommended" that the consistories employ every effort possible to catechize the blacks, for it promised "much good to that unhappy and unenlightened race."[26]

The classis faced a further issue of doctrine and practice in its congregations when one of its consistories asked: "Who are the proper subjects of baptism?" In 1802 classis put the question to the particular synod, which in turn place the request before the General Synod. The 1804 General Synod resolved the question by stating first that the right and privilege of infant baptism does not rest on the full communicant membership of the parents, nor even that either parent be a partaker of the Lord's Supper. So what is to bar a consistory from admitting an infant for baptism? The synod judged that where *both* parents profess errors or heresies or engage in immoral behavior that, were they in full communion, would bar them from the table, then the consistory was to deny baptism. However, if only one parent is guilty of "excommunicable" offenses, the infant is to be baptized on the request of one parent, and only that parent was to present the child for baptism. The synod added one more proviso. Where the minister or an elder found in the parents an ignorance of the "first principles" of the faith, the consistory was likewise to withhold baptism until the parents can be instructed "frequently and affectionately." Thus, the parents could make their vows "with knowledge, sincerity, and truth."[27]

The question didn't go away however. In 1815, a consistory asked the classis: "Is it the duty of a Consistory to enquire into & be satisfied of the Piety of a Parent before they admit his child for baptism?" The classis responded by referring to the 1804 action of the General Synod, which, they added, together with the articles of the church and most particularly Scripture, provides for an affirmative answer. The particular synod, in reviewing the classis's minutes, noted that this question occasioned differing views and so passed the matter back to the General Synod. The 1816 General Synod responded with its judgment that the classis had erred. The synod action of 1804 does not answer the question *explicitly* in the affirmative, claimed the 1816 synod. It went on, then, to recommend that ministers and consistories not admit to baptism the children of parents who "do not manifest evidences, from which, according to the judgment of charity, it may be concluded that they possess faith and piety."[28] In this instance the classis did not hesitate to take cognizance of faith and practice. The local consistory looked beyond itself for advice to the greater church, gathered first in classis. The classis did not act on its own but entered a larger arena, engaging in tug and pull as the matter reached resolution.

In matters of visitation and preaching from the catechism, and in mediating a question about baptism, we see the classis exercising its authority through persuasion. Those ground rules changed when it came to discipline. The congregations and consistories existed within a discipline. The classis could act firmly when necessary, as it in 1801 in a case from the Nistiguana (Niskayuna) church.

The Nistiguana consistory had been embroiled in a dispute with its pastor, John Demarest. Demarest demanded payment from the consistory for money he expended to clear some land. The consistory refused, relying in part on a legal opinion it had received. A newly elected consistory refused to take office until the dispute was cleared up. In the meantime, the congregation elected several "overseers."[29] The classis ruled that the consistory elected by the congregation in 1796 and 1797 could not be considered ecclesiastically as rulers in the church. And since those chosen to replace them refused to serve, the church was to be considered in a state of disorganization. The elders and deacons elected in 1796 and 1797 attempted to resume their offices. The classis ruled that they were illegal and any actions taken by them invalid. The classis subsequently recommended that the church hold a new election of consistory members as soon as possible. The classis further urged the congregation to "study the things that make for peace."

The classis resolution was not well received, and in February of the following year, the congregation asked the classis to reconsider its action. The classis agreed to reconsider, but then refused to overturn the action. Dirck Romeyn, of the nearby Schenectady church, protested the classis's action as "illegal and unconstitutional" and "dangerous to the peace and happiness of the church."[30]

The classis also found itself implicated in the relation between the consistories and their ministers. This can be seen in the strongly controverted issue between the pastor of the Albany church, John Bassett, and the consistory. Bassett had come to Albany in 1787 primarily to lead the newly organized Academy of the Dutch Church. He was a man of no insignificant talent. He had produced a version of the psalms for liturgical use; he had translated theological works from both Dutch and French; and the General Synod had appointed him as a professor of Hebrew. However, he found himself embroiled in a variety of controversies, including calling a minister to preach in Dutch to those still longing to hear the mother tongue in the sanctuary.

One of the more strongly felt issues was his extemporaneous style of delivering sermons. Those who desired the more measured and eloquent sermonizing possible with manuscript preaching were decidedly unhappy. However, the smoldering embers of controversy burst into full flame when it was discovered that Bassett had been urging potential candidates to refuse any call to the Albany church since Albany was not congenial to ministry. The consistory unanimously voted to dissolve the relation. Bassett did not consent; and the classis refused to approve the dissolution.[31]

The consistory appealed the decision to the particular synod of 1804. The synod began its deliberation by declaring that a classis is competent to dissolve a relation between a congregation and its minister on "principles of expediency." The synod then sustained the appeal for two reasons. First, the charge from the consistory against its minister was within the cognizance of the classis and the classis had the power to act. Second, by refusing to act, the classis denied the consistory the opportunity to be heard before the proper ecclesiastical tribunal.

The classis appealed the synod's decision. The classis cited church order to the effect that the consistory should have treated this as a case of discipline against its minister. In that case, the consistory should first have treated the case as a private matter to be worked out between the consistory and Bassett. If that failed to produce resolution, the consistory was then to remove him from office and then present the matter to the classis for final resolution. That hadn't happened.

But the classis offered a second reason. If a pastoral connection could be dissolved for reason of "expediency," what was to restrain a consistory from pursuing a dissolution for any pretext whatsoever? The classis argued that ministers would become so worried about protecting their standing that they would neglect their pastoral duties.

Meanwhile, in December, 1814, Bassett agreed to leave the Albany church. He would leave only on the condition, however, that the church provide him with a lifetime pension.[32] He then moved a few miles up the Hudson to assume the pulpit at the Boght church. That didn't end the affair, however. The particular synod noted the following year that Bassett still had not been prosecuted. That left the charges against him still outstanding. Rumors continued, and he had neither been convicted nor exonerated.

Nor indeed had matters quieted in the Albany church. Several members, led by the well-known and highly influential Stephen Van Renssalaer, petitioned the classis to establish a new congregation in Albany under the name "The Associate Reformed Dutch Church of the city of Albany and the town of Watervliet." The classis refused and the synod concurred, stating that it could see no reason for starting a new congregation.

Nor was the synod finished with the classis. It discerned the Bassett affair behind the application for a new congregation. It was true, as the classis contended, that Bassett had received and accepted a call in good order. Still, the synod enjoined the classis to inquire into the charges against Bassett.

The affair dragged on. The 1806 synod, already irritated at the sloppy state of the classis's minutes, was further unhappy that the classis reported the charges against Bassett dropped. The synod once again instructed the classis either to investigate the charges thoroughly or to produce satisfactory evidence that the charges were withdrawn as "false and unfounded."

Classis went back to work and reported to the 1807 synod that it had taken cognizance of the charges and noted that some were serious indeed. But again it argued that the consistory had withdrawn its charges, and, furthermore, the relation between Bassett and the church had been correctly dissolved and that he had regularly received and accepted a call to a new charge. Life was peaceful in both the Albany and the Boght congregations. The classis added that "to take up reports of such old date on mere *fama clamosa* and to trace them or seek after accusers would be unwarranted and not for edification but on the contrary excite fresh feelings & dissensions which have most happily subsided and been healed."

The particular synod wasn't any happier with this report than it had been in previous year and consequently rejected it. However, this did not sit well with some delegates, and the synod voted to reconsider its action. A further motion to accept the classis action then failed. The synod arrived at compromise by voting to admonish the classis for failing to comply with the injunctions of the synod and thus acting against "all order and good government." But since the classis had not acted within the constitutional time limit of one year and four months, and since all was going well in both churches, the synod judged that it would not further the peace and welfare of the church to keep the matter alive. There the matter ended.[33]

A note must be added in a response from the General Synod. As mentioned, the classis had appealed the particular synod's ruling. In 1806, the General Synod had responded to the question of whether a classis had the power to dissolve a pastoral relation on the grounds of expediency, "though one of the parties be averse from it," in the affirmative. The case was to come before the General Synod, but the classis requested postponement because one of the appellants was ill. In 1809, when the General Synod got around to the matter once again, it repealed its previous reply. No, a classis could not dissolve a pastoral relation for reasons of expediency "because unconstitutional and of an evil tendency, calculated to foster strife in congregations, to encourage worldly-minded professors, to excite animosities in a church against ministers, and repugnant to the practice of the Reformed Dutch Church in all ages."[34]

The case displays not only an early instance of discipline, but it shows the classis, the particular synod, and the consistories working out their relationships within the order of the church. The story was muddied by the agreement between Bassett and the church. The classis needed to find a way to handle a messy "divorce," as well as to investigate rumors against one of its ministers. Through it all, it struggled, along with the particular synod, to function within order. And it was the *classis* that made the final determination.

These early years found the classis also working out its responsibilities in the reception of ministers and in the ordination of candidates to the ministry. As early as 1806, the Beaver Dam consistory petitioned General Synod for a dispensation for David Devoe. This dispensation went directly from the congregation to the General Synod. The synod agreed to the request and referred Devoe to the Albany Classis and instructed the classis to examine him and either to license him or to "appoint a course of private studies" agreeable to Article 8 of church government. Article 8 provided that on approval of the General Synod, the classes were to examine and to provide for remedial instruction left to the classes for their discretion.[35]

Three years later, the 1809 General Synod received a request for indulgence for Teunis Van Vechten of Albany. He had studied theology with a Dr. Mason, a professor of theology in the Associate Reformed Church, a sister denomination. The synod recognized documents from that sister synod and agreed that when Van Vecthen produced a certificate, he was to be admitted to examination by the Classis of Albany. However, in granting the dispensation with two others that came before the synod, the synod added "It is expressly understood that this is not to be construed into a precedent." As soon as the theological school in New Brunswick is in operation "such indulgence shall thereafter cease."[36]

At this time, the establishment of the theological professorate was very much at issue in the denomination. The classis had held the power of ordination for some time. Indeed, it exhibited concern for the quality of its ministers. As early as 1803 it voted that at every future examination, "strictest attention" was to be given to the student's facility in the Hebrew language. In fact, the student was to produce a certificate from a professor of Hebrew testifying to proficiency.[37] However, the responsibility of the classes to candidates was still developing and would reach conclusion by 1820.

The Explanatory Articles (Art. 40) left it to the discretion of the student to apply either to the General Synod or to a classis of his choosing for examination. However, the candidate was required to be examined by the classis within which bounds he had been called, or by the General Synod. The choice was again left to the candidate. In 1813, the Particular Synod of New York requested the General Synod to advise students to apply for the examination for licensure to the classis where they reside as a member of a church of that same classis. The General Synod *recommended* that students apply for examination and licensure to the classis within whose bounds they resided immediately prior to entering theological study.

The General Synod's reply did not satisfy the Classis of Albany. In 1818, the classis proposed a new arrangement:

1st The students shall be received into the Theological College on the recommendation of the respective classes.

2nd every student shall put himself under the care of the Classis to which the Congregation of which he is a member belongs, to be transferred only by an act of said Classis, or the Genl. Synod.

3d A Classis on becoming satisfied of the talents, attainments and views of any applicant shall recommend him to the Professors; and may from time to time during vacations assign him such probationary exercises as shall not interfere with the studies at the College.

4th When the students have completed their course of study, they shall return with the proper credentials to their respective Classes for examination and licensure.

5th Students not belonging to the Dutch Church may apply for admission into the College immediately to the Professors.

The classis saw benefits to the seminary, to the students, and to the classis in this new arrangement. It would benefit the seminary by publicizing the work of the seminary: "much as it may surprise the people of New Brunswick and its vicinity, it is nevertheless a fact that in some of our remote congregations there are many who have never heard of the *existence* of the seminary...." The arrangement would benefit students by providing a bond that both cared for them and taught them respect for the classis. And it would benefit the classes by removing jealousies among the classes, by making classis meetings more interesting, and perhaps most importantly, by helping supply the vacancies of various pulpits.

The General Synod agreed and recommended the amendment of the Explanatory Articles to the effect that the student must return to the classis of origin for licensure and ordination, unless the classis allow the student to be examined by another classis.[38] The circle was complete. In breaking away from the Classis of Amsterdam, the General Synod had reserved to itself a great deal of power in the examination of students for ministry. By the action of 1819/20, the synod returned the power to the classes. Students could no longer choose the classis for their examination, nor could they displace their exam to the General Synod. Albany, which had shown concern for the education of its students, became, with other classes, the "gatekeeper" to the office of minister of the Word.

In a related issue, it has already been noted that the Reformed churches weren't quite sure what to do with ministers from outside their bounds, with "foreign ministers." The classis had had to deal with a German pastor in Schoharie in 1786 and with Paige in Schagticoke in 1792. The issue didn't disappear. In 1803, the Particular Synod of Albany established as policy that the classes were to admit no one who did not have full and recent credentials from an acknowledged "orthodox body" and would profess his agreement with the "doctrines of grace as taught in our churches" and could certify his ministerial standing in said body. The classis must also examine the candidate for his knowledge of didactic and practical theology and the biblical languages. The classis "highly approved" the particular synod's action and ordered its consistories "strictly to conform." That this may have been a problem already in the classis is indicated by its further instruction to provide the delegate from the Beaver Dam consistory with a copy of the particular synod's action. This may have become a bit embarrassing when the particular synod of 1804 rescinded its action of the previous year.[39]

But the issue remained alive throughout the century. The General Synod of 1806 took action on ministers both from other denominations within the country and on foreign ministers. That synod had allowed that a consistory could invite ministers to its pulpit whose character and standing were unknown, provided that the consistory receive a certificate of the minister's good standing from a recognized body. It was a different matter when it came to foreign ministers, however. In such cases, a consistory could not invite the minister into its pulpit until he presented his credentials before the classis. The classis was required to obtain a certificate of licensure, ordination, and dismissal from a competent judicatory as well as letters of recommendation from a "known and respectable character" in the country of the candidate's origin certifying his credentials, good character, and that he adhered to the "doctrines of grace professed by the Reformed Church."[40]

This protective function of the classis grew to such importance that a series of resolutions "concerning foreign ministers" was entered into the front of the minute book of the classis (1818-1822) immediately following the Rules of Order. The resolutions show how the classis raised a wall of protection around its churches:

1. No licentiate or ordained minister could be received into the classis until he had been examined in the presence of the deputatus.[41] The classis had to satisfy itself as to his piety, soundness in faith, and to his adherence to the doctrines and discipline of the Reformed church.

2. Any candidate judged by the classis to have become ordained by another body to allow an easier admission into the Reformed church than the route required of its own candidates was to be disqualified and to be admitted only by the dispensation of the General Synod.

3. Every candidate was required to have spent an equal amount of time in preparation for ministry as was required of Reformed candidates, and any deficiency was to be made up by study in New

Brunswick.

4. When a church became vacant within the classis, the classis would provide the church with a list of licentiates from New Brunswick and would strongly urge the church to use the services of Reformed candidates.

5. The classis would provide vacant churches with supply preachers on request of a consistory, thus "preventing the disorganizing influence of casual & indiscriminate ministrations."

6. No foreign ministers could be received on private letters of introduction or recommendation, but had to present full ecclesiastical credentials.

7. Every foreign minister would be required to spend a full year of probation under the supervision of the classis, and after that year was to present testimonials and to undergo examination by the classis.

The outlines of the classis as institution have grown clearer as the classis and the synods felt their way into its new order in a new era. No story illustrates this as well as the story of the Canadian churches in the Classis of Albany. However, the story stands on its own as well.

II
The Canadian Experiment

It has been noted that when the General Synod reorganized the classes in 1800, it gave Albany Classis charge over those churches formed in Canada until they be sufficiently independent to form their own classis. Albany probably got the nod because far as it was from the Canadian border, it was closest to the "field." As it turned out, the Canadian churches disappeared from the Reformed church by 1820. However, they provided the scene of the first mission endeavor by the Reformed church, with the Albany Classis at the center of the action. It would be a frustrating attempt, which clearly displayed the weakness of this European church on the edge of the frontier.

In 1784, loyalists to the British crown had fled the Mohawk Valley to the region along Lake Ontario's northern shore, stretching fifty miles from Kingston to Belleville. They established four townships. The fourth township, Adolphustown, became home for loyalists who had moved from the Hudson Valley area around Albany. In all, about 2,500 loyalists settled this region, called Upper Canada.[1]

It is at this point that Robert McDowall enters the story, and it's around this remarkable man that the story turns. The Classis of Albany licensed McDowall in 1790, and he soon left for a mission to Canada. He spent the summer forming several congregations, including churches at Ernestown, Fredericksburg, and Adolphustown, from which he was to receive a call. He did not, however, return to Canada until 1798, after the classis had ordained him in 1797. In the meantime, about 1796, the classis had circulated a petition to raise funds from its churches to support missionaries to "visit settlements remote from the body of our Church." These monies were to be the beginning of the mission effort to Canada.

McDowall's efforts were prodigious indeed. The only pastor in Upper Canada, he later recalled that while he spent the majority of his time in the towns to which he had been called, he would travel eastward toward the St. Lawrence 98 miles until 1811, and westward to Toronto 186 miles until 1819. As he calculated it, his work extended 282 miles, within which boundaries there were three ministers from the Church of England, two Lutheran ministers, four Baptists, and a variety of Methodists.[2]

In 1801, the Particular Synod of Albany noted that the congregation at Elizabethtown had no one to supply its pulpit. The synod referred the matter to Albany Classis to take action as early as possible. McDowall reported that several settlements in Canada were anxious to be formed into congregations. The synod conferred on him the power to form churches and instructed him to report to the Classis of Albany.[3] It is not clear that the synod had that power to confer. The Explanatory Articles, article 39, expressly granted the power to form new congregations to the classes.

It appears that the classis did little, and when the synod met the following year, it sent William Ames, a candidate in the Albany Classis, to the Elizabethtown church and to any other congregation that McDowall might direct him. Again in 1803, the synod sent Henry Ostrander, pastor at the Coxsackie church, to Canada for at least six months and instructed the classis to supply his pulpit during his absence.[4]

It wasn't as though the classis wasn't trying. In April, 1803, it instructed John Bassett to correspond with the particular synod of New York to recruit someone to undertake a mission to Canada. Bassett was further detailed to approach the General Synod for funding for the operation. Furthermore, the classis established a committee with full powers to attend to all concerns of the church in Canada.[5] Still, they made little headway. Thus, in May 1804, the General Synod got into the act. The synod reported that neither the classis nor the particular synod had been able to provide missionaries, and suggested the necessity of appointing missionaries and compensating them as well as supplying the pulpits should the missionaries be settled pastors. The synod also recommended that the particular synod appoint a committee to procure missionaries—and then appointed the Classis of Albany as that committee.[6] Still the classis made little progress. In 1806, McDowall wrote to the General Synod that the situation was growing ever more dire. He was one against the forces of an irreligion which was gaining ground despite the longing of many for the gospel. Furthermore, he indicated that both in York and in a settlement on the Bay of Quinte, the inhabitants desired the formation of a church. Elizabethtown, which had been a respectable congregation, was in danger of extinction. McDowall reported that he had often traveled in this extended country preaching six to nine times a week, but his "constitution is now much debilitated, owing to the abundance of his ministerial labors." Worse yet, he warned that the lack of ministers meant a weakening of the congregations' ability to support a minister, and the consequent likelihood the Baptists and others will rend the congregations into so many sects that they won't be able to support a minister of any denomination.[7]

The synod replied that it now had three missionaries ready to leave for Canada, Christian Bork, Conrad Ten Eyck, and Peter Froeligh. The synods of Albany and New York between them contributed about six hundred dollars for the mission. The General Synod also established "The Standing Committee of Missions for the Reformed Dutch Church in America" from ministers and elders in the Synod of Albany. The first organized mission body of the denomination was to be quartered in Albany.

The three missionaries set out in August, 1806. They traveled north across the St. Lawrence, then turned west at the town of Aussenburgh, about seventy miles west of Montreal, crossed back into the United States at Niagara, and returned east along the Mohawk to Albany. Their mission lasted eleven weeks. They reported that during this time they preached seventy-two sermons and organized five churches: Aussenburgh, Williamsburgh, Matilda, a church twenty-five miles north of York, and one in Markham, northeast of York. In addition, they re-established the church in Elizabethtown.[8]

The standing committee was next able to find missionaries for Canada in 1809, when it sent Henry Ostrander (who had been to Canada in 1803) and Jacob Sickles. They returned with a sobering report: "...the number who have experienced the power of religion, is small indeed." But they were received with kindness and found reason to hope.

It is our decided opinion however, that this can only be effected by Ministers who are willing to settle in the Province, and that soon. In two or three places the people think themselves able to afford a preacher a competent support, and they are anxiously looking for an opportunity to make a trial. It is probable that they find themselves mistaken; but with some assistance they would be able to raise sufficient support.[9]

Sickles reported to the particular synod the need for ministry of word and sacrament in the Canadian churches, and the synod appointed a committee of John Bradford of Albany and Cornelius Bogardus of Schenectady to write to candidates and ministers who might possibly desire to settle in Canada, and if they were to find them, to settle them immediately.[10]

The standing committee was able to employ a missionary, John Beattie, to travel through Upper Canada in 1810. He reported that he spent eighteen weeks, preached fifty-three sermons, baptized nineteen, received sixteen members by confession and two by certificate. In addition, he organized a church in York which came under the care of Albany Classis. The General Synod received his report in June, 1812. The synod considered Canada to be an "open field" for mission but added, "whether it would be expedient to send missionaries to Canada under existing circumstances, must be left discretionary with the Standing Committee on Missions." It is to be remembered that war had broken out between Britain and the United States, a factor of no small importance in the success of this experiment.[11]

After the war, the standing committee heard from McDowall in 1815 that while prospects had declined during the war, things were looking up once again. Elizabethtown had found a stated supply, another missionary had found his way to Canada, and McDowall himself had visited the settlements once or twice a year to administer baptism.[12]

The 1816 General Synod spent its entire time in consideration of mission on the Canadian churches. It reflected that if the Canadian churches were not neglected, they "might soon become respectable, and be an important addition to the Reformed Dutch Church." At the same meeting, McDowall requested that the standing committee send him "one of the best commentaries on the Bible." The committee deemed that since he hadn't received adequate compensation for his work, his request was reasonable and it recommended that the synod purchase and send him Scott's Commentary on the Bible (It turned out that McDowall had in the meantime obtained a copy of Scott's Commentary. The synod voted to send him the money anyway, or at least some books as an equivalent. He chose the books).[13]

Later that same year, McDowall reported that he had found a man "pious, orthodox, well informed," Abraham Wright, who desired to be licensed and ordained. The classis considered this sort of ordination to be a departure from the established rules requiring a dispensation from the General Synod. The classis requested advice from the particular synod, who referred the question to General Synod. The General Synod of 1817 looked favorably on the request. It would probably be "the means of establishing a Classis in the Province of Upper Canada." Judging the case "remarkably singular," the synod was prepared to depart from established rule. It authorized Wright to apply to the Classis of Albany for examination and authorized the classis to license him."[14]

At the same meeting of the particular synod in 1816, the classis petitioned the synod to advocate for a theological school within the bounds of the Synod of Albany. The classis's particular concern was the areas to the north and west of Albany as well as, most particularly, the churches in Canada. The classis argued that the shortage of ministers resulted in the loss of some churches to the Reformed church. The classis agreed that it would be difficult financially, but it expressed hope, adding that it didn't seem to be making much progress raising funds for New Brunswick anyway. The General Synod was to hear nothing of the plan. So far as the synod could see, the classis had no practical plans to fund the school, another seminary would jeopardize the New Brunswick Seminary, and the project was likely to lead to strife and division within the Reformed church.[15]

By 1817, the standing committee was bringing a mixed report to the General Synod. The Canadian churches were in a deplorable condition, but there was modest hope. A minister of the Associate Reformed church was about to settle in Canada with hopes of joining the Reformed Dutch church. The ordination of Wright would provide a third minister for Canada, thus making it possible for a classis finally to be constituted. However, there were other doubts. Did the General Synod have the resources to continue its efforts in Canada when demands were growing closer to home? The committee detailed extensive vacancies in churches in the United States. Classis Montgomery, for example, complained of ten or twelve vacancies. Still, should the Canadian churches form a classis, there was hope that they could send prospective candidates to New Brunswick who would then return to Canada to supply their churches. The supply problem could be solved by growing their own ministers![16]

The doubts present in this report became grave when the standing committee reported to the General Synod of 1818 that it was "impressed with a strong conviction that the Canada missions are not productive of good effects which ought to be the object of missionary labours. What other missionary ground can be occupied to greater advantage, is a point which the committee deem it their duty to submit for decision to the collective wisdom of the Church." The General Synod wasn't prepared to go quite that far. They received the report of John Schermerhorn and Jacob Van Vechten, missionaries who had traveled through Canada in 1817. The two had reported eleven churches in Canada: Matilda, Osnaburgh, Williamsburgh, two in Ernestown, Fredericksburgh, Sophiasburgh, Sydney, and York. The synod still hoped that with the prospect of Cornelius Schermerhorn to settle in Canada and one or more ministers from the Presbyterian church who desired to join the Reformed church, that a classis could yet be formed in Canada. The synod again urged Wright to apply to Albany Classis for examination and directed the Synod of Albany to organize a classis in Upper Canada.[17]

In fact, the February meeting of the classis received a letter from McDowall who named himself, Cornelius Schermerhorn, and W. Jenkins as ready to form themselves into a classis. He also urged the speedy ordination of Wright. The classis agreed. It urged them to form a classis and to report to the Particular Synod in October 1819. It is the last report from Canada. The particular synod's records report no action to this end.

The Canadian churches had taken a different route. They joined in an effort to form a Presbytery of the Canadas, a foundation and forerunner of the Presbyterian Church in Canada. McDowall himself was to become the first moderator of the first Presbyterian synod in Canada.[18]

In the meantime, the General Synod moved the Standing Committee on Missions from Albany to New York in 1818. Under the new dispensation, the committee acted to broaden the cause of mission throughout the church. All classes were to consider themselves as "auxillaries to General Synod" in the cause of domestic missions. The classes were to promote missionary efforts, most especially by appointing agents to solicit subscriptions for missionary purposes, and by taking note of congregations that failed to take offerings for the cause of mission. The standing committee would henceforth report to the General Synod the amount received from each congregation in the cause of mission.[19]

What happened in Canada? John Moir argues plausibly that the War of 1812 provided the signal event. The war was to occasion a new nationalism in Canada. Land there was plentiful and cheap and drew many United States immigrants north. However, ninety percent of the settlers had arrived since the loyalists first came. When war threatened between the U.S. and Britain, the question naturally arose whether new settlers from south of the border would be loyal to their new country. This question was especially acute for the leaders of denominations that had roots in the United States. Would their loyalty lie with Britain or with their original homeland? McDowall and his followers did not hesitate to proclaim loyalty to the crown.[20] The church chose to be Canadian.

Without denying the strength of Moir's thesis, this study has noted other dynamics at work. The Dutch church in the United States had problems finding ministers for its own churches, let alone the new Canadian congregations. But even had it supplied sufficient ministers, its polity made the experiment difficult. Founding churches, electing consistories, calling ministers, and supervising churches all had to be worked through the cumbersome machinery of a classis, in this case across long distances. How was the classis to exercise oversight at that distance? Even so, the Albany Classis, along with the denomination, had embarked on a course of mission and church extension that would carry it through the nineteenth and on into the twentieth century.

III
The Revivalist Impulse
(1820-1850)

The classis reported its "state of religion" in 1831 with these words:

The Classis while they ardently desire that multitudes may be added to the communion of the churches under their care do not think that the amount of piety in them is always to be estimated by the number of those additions. They would rather derive their conclusion of the religious state of the churches from the pious preserving deportment of their members. No church however favored can always live in a state of religious excitement and it is altogether erroneous to conclude after the first favour of religious feeling in new converts has abated that they have less of deep-tuned piety 'tho they do not evince the same extacy of joy, these considerations the Classis believe at the present day are too little regarded, and hence it is not uncommon to hear it said that religion in a church is cold and dead unless an excited state of feeling constantly exist. We trust that among us there are not a few who judging according to the rule which is here suggested are daily affording increased evidence of their conversion to God.[1]

With this muted approval the classis greeted the arrival of a new religious awakening in Albany. The classis represented a church that could accept evangelical fervor; it was, after all, the church of the Freylinghuisens. But its acceptance could not be wholehearted. It is the burden of this chapter to show why this is

37

so.

Nathan Hatch describes the period from the turn of the nineteenth century until well into that same century as a time of the emergence of a deep democratic impulse on the American religious landscape. He outlines three features of the popular religious movements of the early nineteenth century: a denial of the distinctions that set the clergy apart as a separate order; the empowering of ordinary people by "taking their deepest spiritual impulses at face value rather than subjecting them to the scrutiny of orthodox doctrine and the frowns of respectable clergymen"; and a lack of cognizance of limits among the nascent religious movements.[2] It was the most "centrifugal epoch" in American church history. "It was a time when the momentum of events pushed toward the periphery and subverted centralized authority and professional expertise."[3]

This era of ferment allowed the common folk to "scorn tradition, relish novelty and experimentation, grope for fresh sources of authority, and champion an array of millenial schemes, each in its own way dethroning heirarchy and static religious forms."[4] Within a "sea of sectarian rivalries," little happened in the way of discipline outside a variety exercised in local churches. Denominations maintained authority by seldom exercising it.[5]

It was a time when new churches—and movements that made little pretention of becoming church—could spring up as quickly as folk could gather and appoint a preacher. He (or she) need not be educated; in fact his (or her) education could count against him. While the example may be extreme (and only somewhat marginal), the Mormons reported that on several occasions a man heard a discourse, was baptized, confirmed, received a call, and was sent on a mission, all on the same day![6]

Revival in Albany

This ferment was to take Albany by storm in the late 1820s. David Hackett has argued that the First Great Awakening largely by-passed Albany. There was little evangelicalism in early Albany.[7] It must be remembered, though, that the Albany church had had Theodorus Frelinghuysen as pastor in the mid-eighteenth century. Son of a leader of the awakening in the

Raritan Valley of New Jersey, he could hardly have left his congregation unaware of the attraction of a more evangelical expression of the ancient faith. However, Albany at the turn of the nineteenth century was a town where the British and the Dutch had learned to live together. Hackett even argues that the Dutch may well have welcomed the Revolution not as opportunity to greater liberty, but as an occasion for the restoration of the traditional order in the city.[8] The coming of a new class of workers who would be receptive of the new tenets of American individualism was yet to come. In fact, Hackett shows that in 1817 the two Dutch and the four Presbyterian congregations accounted for nearly two-thirds of Albany's church membership. Furthermore, more than two-thirds of those members were to be found in the top two deciles of the 1817 tax list.[9]

In the 1820s, Albany began to welcome large numbers of journeymen, petty shopkeepers, and laborers, mostly from western New England. This population was most receptive to any ideology or faith that promised greater autonomy, and they provided fertile ground for a new religious awakening.[10]

The Rev. Edward Norris Kirk, a pastor in Albany's Second Presbyterian Church, had been caught up in the revivals of Princeton and Yale of the 1820s. In 1828 he began to advocate a more evangelical style in that church. The consequent agitation resulted in a split and the subsequent establishment of the Fourth Presbyterian Church. His new group gathered in a hall over an old tannery in a poor section of the city in the northern suburbs. There they held constant meetings. Churchgoers heard a new doctrine that challenged fixed Calvinist orthodoxy: "The new Christian message heard in this room [over the tannery] denied the doctrine of innate depravity and thereby tied Christian thinking closer to the new society's more reasonable commitment to human ability. The belief in predestination was replaced by a more tangible confidence in the human will."[11]

This was the first of a number of new evangelical churches that would soon predominate in Albany. Between 1828 and 1836 these evangelicals moved from a minority of twenty-five percent of the population to a majority of fifty-four percent. In sheer numbers, they would grow from 592 members in 1828 to 2,407 in 1836 for the congregations for which statistics are available. By comparison, what Hackett calls the "established churches" grew from 1,813 in 1828 to 2,092 in 1836.[12]

Reformed Response

The Reformed response, as cited above, was qualified approval. The 1831 classis report on the state of religion was authored by John Ludlow, pastor of Albany's First Church. Ludlow had been a professor of Biblical Literature in New Brunswick from 1817-1823, during the tenure of John Livingstone's presidency and professorship. Livingstone himself had come under the sway of evangelicalism. James Van Hoeven comments that a generation of students would have heard Livingstone relate the story of his own conversion. Students at New Brunswick formed prayer cells, Bible study groups, and a missionary society under Livingstone's tenure.[13]

Furthermore, James Cannon began lecturing in pastoral theology in 1826. His *Lectures on Pastoral Theology,* published in 1853, contained the substance of his earlier teaching. His book included a chapter on revivals, subtitled "Pastoral Vigilance in Seasons of General Awakenings and Enlargement of the Church." In it, he allowed that God, through the Spirit, could impart his influence in "refreshing drops, or in gentle and insinuating dews of the night, or in abundant rains, according to the good pleasure of his will."[14] He was cautious of a "feverish religion which must have a *stir* around it," but which was not a "sound state of mind."[15] He warned his pastors-in-training that a "great excitement may be *a great trial* of the hearts of men, on which they may fail, grieve the Holy Spirit in various ways, and exhibit little improvement." This fact, he added, serves to "explain to us *how religion has come to decline soon*...immediately after a great awakening has occurred...."[16] Cannon went on to caution his listeners not to be in too much of a hurry to receive new members from the revivals. In fact, he reflected on the "new measures" and baldly stated, "*For no useful purpose is there a necessity* for anxious-meetings."[17] His was a cautionary acceptance of revivals, always careful to guard the priority of God who, through the Spirit, authored revival and conversion. Pastors trained in this language could accept the revivals, but only on condition.

The arrival of the revivals in Albany evoked further difficulties that had been in the wind not far distant in the Reformed church. In 1820, meeting in special session at Albany, the particular synod gathered to hear the appeal of the case of Conrad Ten Eyck against the Classis of Montgomery. Ten Eyck had been accused of preaching the doctrine of unlimited atonement. The case against Ten Eyck surfaced a fear of Hopkinsianism among the Reformed. Samuel Hopkins (1721-1805) had been a student and friend of Jonathan Edwards. He became a leader in the New England theology, a sort of mild Calvinism that emphasized the freedom of the will more than had Edwards and thus modified the doctrines of original sin, election, and atonement.[18]

Van Hoeven claims that it was a fear of Hopkinsianism behind the General Synod's action in 1814 that cautioned the classes against easy admission of congregational ministers into their ranks.[19] The Particular Synod of Albany had noted with disapproval that the Montgomery Classis had received a candidate from the Congregational church without examination. They requested a judgment from the General Synod. That synod found Montgomery's practice "very improper and highly censurable." The synod worried about a form of government very different from the Reformed "which government we believe to be according to the word of God." But more, "it is believed that that body" holds to doctrines contrary to "many of those which we believe to be the pure unadulterated doctrines of the gospel."[20] This is a worry directed toward New England.

While little primary source material is available on the Albany Classis's response to the impending crisis in the Reformed church,[21] Albany could hardly been unaware of what was going on. After all, the synod met in their city, and they sent delegates to the meeting. Indeed, such intensity of feeling did the case arouse, one can hardly expect the ecclesiastical populace to be blase.

Furthermore, the source material at hand provides some evidence of tremors in Albany. The Particular Synod of Albany's minutes of 1824 quote Albany Classis's report that "in the church at Bethlehem, notwithstanding the endeavors made by some persons to promote schism, peace and prosperity are seen to prevail...."[22] What was going on in Bethlehem? The affair with Ten Eyck had exploded into full-scale schism in the Reformed church. Churches and ministers in Montgomery joined with others from the Hackensack area in New Jersy to form the True Reformed Dutch Church (TRDC) in 1822. The leader of the New Jersey schism was one Solomon Froeligh. His daughter married Ralph Westervelt, who was to become pastor of the Bethlehem congregation. He had left Bethlehem for Wynantskill in 1815. However, one of the elders who served during his stay at Bethlehem, Storm Vander Zee, was to become one of the first officers of the Bethlehem TRDC when it formed in 1827.[23] Furthermore, the Wynantskill TRDC was to form soon after Westervelt died in Wynantskill ("while preparing to secede," according to Corwin[24]). Evidently "peace and prosperity" in Bethlehem was little more than a temporary truce.

Other tremors of the fear or response to alleged Hopkinsianism are evident in the case of the examination of candidates in the classis. As early as 1818, the particular synod had raised questions about William Ames. He had been accused of "Arminian tendencies." The classis examined Mr. Ames, and found themselves satisfied.[25] (Ames, it is to be recalled, had been sent as a missionary to Canada in 1804!)

A more serious case appears to have arisen with the call of the churches at Rotterdam on Jeremiah Searle. Thomas Romeyn lodged a dissent against the call with the particular synod. Romeyn was troubled that Searle had expressed difficulty with the eternal generation of the second person of the Trinity, problems with the atonement of Christ for his people, and had also found it hard to accept the representative character of Adam in the covenant of works. The deputatus reported to the synod that it was true, Searle was vague and indeed held to "doctrines different from our own." But he had made explanation to the satisfaction of the classis and with that had changed the votes of some who would otherwise have voted against him. The synod, of course, had no access to those explanations and thus recommended no course of action. They did, however, suggest the propriety of the several classes guarding against the introduction of errors and called on them to "contend earnestly for the faith once delivered to the saints."[26]

This was not an isolated instance. In 1829 the classis fretted over the examination of a Henry Mandeville who had applied for licensure. The classis recorded "a matter of regret...that Mr. Mandeville's mind labors on the doctrine of the eternal generation or Sonship of Jesus Christ neither believing nor disbelieving the doctrine." Again, one detects a nervousness over the threat of Unitarianism encroaching from the "east," New England. Remarkably this time, however, the classis received no explanation from Mandeville but voted licensure because it "apprehended that a subscription of the formula given in the standards of our church will sufficiently guard against any evils which might be supposed to result out of his licensure."[27] One can only speculate that the classis either expected that by coming under its discipline, Mandeville would have to answer for any heretical doctrines, or that by signing the formula he was disavowing his recusal on the doctrine in question, notwithstanding what he might have stated in his examination.

If the examination of candidates shows the classis defending its doctrinal flanks, what then of its response to the evangelical tenor of its time? The city of Albany was, after all, smack in the middle of a revival. A review of the reports on the state of religion displays the classis alert to the spirit of the time and could record real growth in numbers of converts. While in 1830, the classis would lament of "no extensive outpourings of the Spirit," the churches did report weekly lectures, Bible classes, and meetings for social prayer, all methods in the new spirit of revival.[28]

By 1832, however, the classis could boast some positive growth. That year it recorded 444 accessions by confession of faith. It is notable, however, that the greatest increase happened outside the city: Westerlo reported 102, Coxsackie 88, Union 46, Second Berne 42, and Salem 34.[29] The following year, the increases had dwindled to 153 but remained real. Again the growth was outside the city: 41 in Bethlehem, 17 in both Coxsackie and Union, and 16 in both Salem and Gibbonville.[30]

Some of the language of the revivals surfaces again in 1840 when the classis reported both that "some of the churches deplore the spiritual dearth which has prevailed among them and lament that they have not participated in the refreshing from the presence of the Lord, that has been in many places delightfully enjoyed," and that "other churches, however, we rejoice to say, have been blessed with the presence of the Holy Spirit & very encouraging accessions have been made to their numbers."[31] By 1843 the classis could again report that "many churches have been highly favored by the Lord, by the outpouring of his Spirit...." This time the increase included the Albany churches, First reporting 59, Second 129, and Third 64.[32] In fact, by the following year the classis was happy to claim that the converts of the previous year had held steady: "The grapes of a former vintage have not proved wild grapes," and "While [during the year past] there have been no revivals of religion as they are called, or general outpourings of the Spirit (as they might more properly be named) still the churches have not relapsed into the langour of former years. Facts show that past wakenings were not the mere ebullitions of excited feeling, but on the contrary the steady & progressive increase of communicants, in connection with their steadfast adherence to holiness...."[33]

These reports on the state of religion occasion three comments. First, while the churches could report real growth, the numbers were hardly of the sort that the revival churches in Albany could boast (see Hackett's numbers above, p. 6111). Second, in both language and caution, the classis reflected a theological interpretion of events that Cannon was proferring at New Brunswick. But third, the language and tone of the reports reflected the evangelical concerns of the age. The classis would "speak this language" in its reports well through the end of the nineteenth century.

A Nondemocratic Clergy

Nor was the explicit mention of revivals the only response to the spirit of the democratizing era. Hatch's comment that this was a time of the democratic leveling of the clergy has already been cited. He cites Timothy Dwight's comments at the Yale commencement of 1814, where Dwight worried about the explosion of illiterate ministers. He denounced those who "declare, both in their language and conduct, that the desk ought to be yielded to the occupancy of Ignorance." Popular preachers like Lorenzo Dow retorted, "I see no gospel law that authorizes any man, or set of men, to forbid, or to put up bars to hinder or stop any man from preaching the gospel."[34]

The classis reflected Dwight's worry and would have none of Dow's freedom to allow anyone who felt so called to step into one of the pulpits in the classis. They were scarcely ready to cede to a new religious ferment that leveled the distinction between clergy and laity. It has already been remarked that Ludlow had served a stint as professor at New Brunswick. He was to leave Albany later to become provost of the University of Pennsylvania, from there to return to New Brunswick in 1852. John De Witt, who had been pastor at the second church in Albany, left to become professor at New Brunswick in 1823 and his successor, Isaac Ferris, was later to become chancellor and professor at New York University. These were hardly men ready to admit to a challenge to clerical professionalism. Moreover, the classis kept its clergy and its churches on a tight reign when it came to who was authorized to preach. This is illustrated not only by the by now well established procedure of examination of candidates for licensure. In 1829, the particular synod had resolved that the classes enforce the twelfth article of church government concerning ministers and secular employment. The relevant article read:

A minister of the word being once lawfully called in a manner beforehand mentioned, is bound to the service of the sanctuary, as long as he liveth. Therefore he shall not be at liberty to devote himself to a *secular vocation*, except for great and important reasons concerning which the classis shall inquire and determine.

Peter Van Zandt, for example, had been a minister without charge in the classis. He had to give up preaching on account of a "throat difficulty" and had become a physician. The classis requested him to appear at the next meeting of the classis "or assign a reason for his present employment."[35]

The problem the Reformed were having with "foreign ministers" continued, perhaps even worsened in this era of revivalism. Two signal cases emerged for the classis in the 1830s. In 1834, the church at Coeymans placed a call upon Thomas Edwards, a minister of the "Independent body of England." The classis discovered that he had not been ordained by the laying on of hands and ordered his ordination. This instance, however, provoked the classis to request of the General Synod's Board of Missions not to appoint foreign ministers who had not been ordained by the laying on of hands. The classis also resolved "that it is inexpedient & fraught with injury for ministers in their individual capacity to give such certificates to foreigners as shall give them access to our churches" and the opportunity of "sealing ordinances before they have been regularly accepted & authorized by some classis." Finally, the classis reminded its consistories not to admit a person of whatever denomination to preach until he presented his credentials to the classis to be accepted and authorized.[36] These worries proved prophetic. In September, 1836, the Coeymans church reported to the classis that Edwards "is not laboring among them." He had abandoned his parish, and they were left without a minister.[37]

The classis however, showed that it was not averse to such foreigners when, again in 1835, it received an application from a John Woods, also described as an Independent minister from England. The classis authorized him to officiate at any vacancy under the care of the classis.[38] Again, however, the experience proved unhappy. He had been installed in Washington and Gibbonville in 1835. In January, 1837, the classis dissolved the relation for "circumstances implicating" his ministerial standing. He had been accused of public intoxication and subsequently confessed to one instance. The classis suspended him for three months.[39] So burned, the classis in 1840 reacted to the General Synod's new rules on foreign ministers: "The Classis have with regret & surprise seen the recommendation of Genl. Synod relating to the invitation of ministers from foreign bodies to preach in our churches, neglected by some of our most respectable churches & consequent settlement of strangers in our churches, where our own sons have been neglected."[40]

Nor, it appears, had the Coeymans church learned from the sad episode with Edwards. The April, 1841, classis frowned on an arrangement made by the Coeymans and New Baltimore church with a new preacher. The classis judged that the churches had acted contrary to the constitution "in inviting or admitting into their pulpit a gentleman licensed by a body not in correspondance with the Dutch church & that it is impossible under the circumstances of the case, without a dispensation from Genl. Synod that he should be settled in the Dutch Church, & that therefore the Classis recommend and enjoin, that consistory shall no longer employ the said gentleman."[41]

The exercise of classical authority over its ministers was not limited to outsiders or to smaller congregations. It has already been noted that Isaac Ferris, pastor of Second, Albany, was a man of considerable stature and influence. In 1833, he received and accepted a call to an Associate Presbyterian church in New York City. At first, Second's consistory had joined in the application for dissolution of pastoral relationship between the church and Ferris. They subsequently discovered that Ferris was to receive a salary of $2,000 from the New York church and canvassed the congregation to raise his salary from $1,650 to match the offer from down state. Despite some hasty and impassioned letters not only from Ferris but from the New York City congregation, the classis denied the request for dissolution, and Ferris remained.[42] One gets a sense of why the classis may have been less than sympathetic to Ferris's "plight" from the state of religion report earlier that year that had congratulated the Union and New Salem congregations for having doubled the salary they were offering a pastor from $300 to $600![43]

Likewise, the classis continued its careful examination of students for ordination. In 1841, the classis included as subjects for examination: didactic and polemical theology, the biblical languages, pastoral theology and church government, and experimental religion. In the last named subject, one can tease out an evangelical emphasis (however, the classis records no examination in the topic and by the following year, the subject had disappeared from the list of examination topics).[44] In 1842, the classis added biblical literacy and sacraments to the list.[45] This is hardly an environment to encourage quick and easy entrance into the ministry.

The issue of ministry, however, did occasion some tension, brought on perhaps by the evangelical spirit of the time. In 1850, the Jerusalem consistory brought to the classis a statement that read:

Whereas we believe that titled distinctions as now conferred in the church upon Ministers of the word of God, are unscriptural as well as unconstitutional, which declares, all ministers of the gospel equal in rank and authority. Art. 1, Sec. 19.

And whereas the title D.D., Doctor of Divinity, which signifies nothing more than a Spiritual Teacher, is conferred on some of the Ministers of the Gospel and not on others, equal Stewards of the Mysteries of God. Therefore,

Resolved that we the consistory of the Church of Jerusalem will in future regard our Minister, as well as all the regularly ordained Ministers of the Church, by their official title D.D. Doctor or Teacher of Divinity: Not as honorary, but as the most appropriate designation of office.[46]

The classis responded by resolving "that the parity of the christian ministry as to rank & authority is a principle clearly recognized both by the scriptures & constitution of the Reformed Dutch Church." Furthermore, using the language of Jerusalem's proposal, the classis further stated that it would "recognize the term Doctor of divinity, in the literal signification as an official designation for all the properly comissioned ministers of Christ."[47]

The action did not go unchallenged. The resolutions were approved by a divided house. Four opposed the resolution, including the ministers of First, Albany, Duncan Kennedy (himself a D.D.), and of Bethlehem, Ralph Willis. They were quick to state on the record that their negative votes were not to be interpreted as a disbelief in the doctrine of the parity of ministry, but that their sole object had been "to oppose the agitation of the subject involved, & especially as the resolution in question is but one of a series of resolutions, the discussion of which they consider useless, & the adoption of which they cannot but regard as uncalled for, inexpedient & injurious."[48] The historical investigator looks longingly and in vain for that "series of resolutions," and indeed for the "subject involved."

However, given the spirit of the age, one can reasonably surmise that lurking behind it all is the tension of the Reformed church's muted acceptance of the evangelical impulse. Thus, a long-accepted Reformed principle of the parity of ministry came up against the democratic tenor of the time. However, the Reformed opposition to a democratic leveling of clergy did not emerge only from the presence of some decidedly "aristocratic" clergy among them. They were "constitutionally" opposed, if you will. The church order that the classis lived out required an oversight of clergy that precluded ordination in the heat of an enthusiastic moment.

Oversight of Congregations

Nor were congregations free to exercise their autonomy by following whatever wind of the Spirit they thought might be in the air. The classis also kept a close eye on their life and activity. The congregations were not free to wander off on their own, discovering revivals where they might fall. The classis required of each consistory a yearly report of the life of the congregation. In 1837, the classis required that a report be recorded in the minutes of each consistory that would include an account of the state of each congregation's life, a report on sabbath schools, on monies raised for benevolent purposes, on prayer meetings, on family visitation, and on the preaching of the Heidelberg Catechism.[49] This list evidences a veritable catalogue of the early nineteenth century concerns of the Reformed church. Furthermore, the classis required consistories to submit their minutes for annual inspection by the classis. Consistories often omitted the required reports. The classis didn't enforce the regulation strictly, but instead used constant reminder to nudge consistories into compliance. When the classis did receive minutes, it inspected them carefully and took them quite seriously. For example, in 1841, on examining the consistory minutes of the Second Church in Albany, it discovered that an elder had resigned and his family had been dismissed for reasons "altogether unsatisfactory" to the consistory. The classis committee reviewing the minutes opined that the reasons for the elder's resignation contained grave charges against the minister, if true. If the charges were untrue, the elder would properly be subject to discipline.[50]

Thus, too, in contrast to what Hatch describes as typical for the American experience of this era in the limitation of discipline to the local congregation, the classis was highly involved in the disciplinary lives of its congregations. The records are replete with instances of discipline. Consistories were required to receive the permission of the classis to excommunicate egregious offenders. But other cases happened as well.

One will suffice as representative. In 1844, two brothers, John Howell Jr. and David B. Howell, members of the Bethlehem congregation, were suspended for using profane language. They appealed their suspension to classis. The classis did not sustain their appeal. However, it did establish a committee to:

convey the confession made by the Appelants, viz., that if under excitement they used any expression inconsistent with christian character, they were truly sorry for it: to the consistory of Bethlehem & convey the opinion of Classis, that on this basis, it will be proper to restore the appellants to their former standing.

Two months later, that committee reported to the classis that the consistory at Bethlehem refused to remove the suspension until the Howells appeared before them. They did not judge the report of their apology in classis as sufficient.[51] The case dragged on, but the point is clear: discipline was a shared affair, between consistory and classis.

The classis was active as well in the relations *between* the churches. In 1837 a Presbyterian church at Onesquethaw applied and received membership in the classis. By 1840 the Union and Salem consistories laid a problem before the classis. Many of their members desired to transfer to the Onesquethaw church, it being closer to their residences. Both the Union and the Salem churches hesitated to comply. They were already weak and could scarcely afford to lose many members. Were they required to honor the requests for transfer? The classis replied that yes, they were to transfer the members. However, the classis also discovered that the Onesquethaw church already included members from Union and Salem on its rolls. Nor was that all. They had ordained some! All this without having received proper letters of transfer. This the classis judged to be "irregular & subversive to the peace & discipline of the church...."[52]

A similar but more nuanced case occurred in a dispute over a request for transfer from the Union to the Jerusalem church. One John Hendrickson wrote to the classis to report that he and his family desired to transfer from the Union church to the Jerusalem church but that the consistory at Union refused. The classis discovered that the Hendricksons had not been attending at Union. Classis urged the Union consistory to appoint a committee to begin discipline against the Hendricksons for neglect of church attendance. However, the classis added, it had no authority to act at this stage. It did later. The consistory at Union suspended the Hendricksons from communion and Hendrickson appealed. On a split vote of nine to seven (with only two ministers voting in the majority) the classis sustained the appeal. Simon Westfall, the pastor at Union, appealed the classis decision to the particular synod. The classis hastened to add that while it had sustained Hendrickson's appeal, it could not condone his actions and that the appeal was upheld solely on the supposition that his request for dismission had been made prior to the commencement of the disciplinary proceedings. As it turned out, the particular synod sustained Westfall's appeal against the classis.[53]

Classis concerns for its congregations were broader than intra- and inter-church disciplinary snags. It displayed a more caring response to churches that faced sometimes rather extreme difficulty, although the classis itself could offer little relief. In 1830, the Second Church of Berne was sending out distress signals. It requested of and received from the classis permission to apply to other churches in the classis for financial assistance.[54] It is noteworthy both that the classis itself neither offered nor solicited aid and that the church found it necessary to request permission to approach other churches. In 1841, Berne was still struggling. This time, the classis approved an application of the Berne church to the denomination's "missionary fund" for assistance of $50.[55] Yet a decade later the Berne church would be back appealing that they had become "unable to maintain the preaching of the gospel." This time the classis was more forthcoming. It proposed that if the church would pay a preacher approved by classis "$125 for one year—when such sum is fully paid or secured to be paid—then this classis will guarantee $75 for one year or proportionally for six months."[56]

The Berne church was not the only one facing financial hardship. The classis noted that as the country was experiencing a severe depression, its churches shared in the difficulty: the churches "have all been more or less affected by the pecuniary embarassments of the times & some of them very seriously & find it difficult to furnish themselves with the means of grace." It appeared that both the Third Church in Albany and the Westerlo church had lost their pastors because they couldn't support them. The classis could do little more than wring its hands and worry that so many churches were vacant. It exhorted the churches to settle ministers as soon as possible. Apparently, that counsel had some effect, for by the September meeting, five churches had issued calls![57]

In two instances, churches "found" new ways to avert serious threat. In April, 1842, the Cohoes church warned the classis that it was in danger of losing its building. The classis could do no more than to grant permission to the church to seek aid from the churches and the individuals in classis. However, by November of the same year, the situation had grown dire. The church reported that the sheriff was about to sell its building. It proposed a solution. If the corporation of the church remained intact, the church's liabilities would remain, and the people would not resubscribe. However, if they dissolved and reorganized, they could avoid liability for debts currently in effect. The church asked the classis whether such a course would be "in agreement with Christian principles." The classis replied, without dissent: "the necessity of the case justifies the course: because the creditors would not be benefitted if the church was abandoned."[58]

The classis had already noted that Third Church in Albany was facing trouble. Third had reported to the classis in 1842 that the church was in danger of having its building sold to repay its debt. In the meantime, it burned down. In the event, the combination of insurance money and the exhortations of its stated supply was such that the congregation emerged better off than before![59]

The discussion seems to have moved some distance from the classis's response to a revivalistic culture. But as it cared for its churches, especially churches not fired by the new wind of evangelical fervor, the classis was responding to the zeitgeist. It valued the life of the ordinary congregation. It knew that the churches could not always live in "a state of religious excitement," but once the "first favour of religious feeling...has abated" churches and believers continue on.

The Culture of Evangelicalism

The Classis of Albany's concern for the life of its churches in the revival context included such issues as temperance, sabbath keeping, sabbath schools, and missions and the like. This concern was not new. The classis had concerned itself with such "social issues" earlier in the century. It is important to note here because it was precisely against some of these concerns that the populist religious movements of the times protested. Hatch notes that populist religious leaders consciously worked against the efforts of Calvinist coalitions to buttress a "Christian civilization." They firmly challenged such Calvinist goals as home and foreign missions, the regulation of sabbath observance, the education of ministers, and the forbidding of Sunday mail. About this time, coalitions of moderate Calvinist leaders formed a number of voluntary associations to extend their influence: American Board of Commissioners for Foreign Missions (1810), the American Home Missionary Society (1826), the American Tract Society (1825), and the American Sunday School Union (1824).[60] The Albany Classis's interest in mission was evident already in its Canadian connection. Further evidence can be found in its August, 1820, meeting where most of the meeting turned on a discussion of mission and resulted in the establishment of a missionary society in the classis.[61] But the 1830 report on the state of religion notes with approval that several churches were contributing to the American Bible Society, most were cooperating with tract distribution, and societies promoting temperance had "with small exception" been organized in every congregation.[62] In 1833, the classis could also report that both the temperance cause and that of sabbath schools were receiving "an increased share of attention" in the churches.[63]

The classis, then, was entering the "Protestant empire" of eighteenth century America. But it was doing so on its own terms.

IV
Into the Empire

The nineteenth century witnessed the emergence of what Martin Marty calls the "righteous empire"—a self-consciously Protestant hegemony of American Christianity.[1] To be a Christian citizen in the United States meant simply that one was a Protestant, most likely of the evangelical subspecies. The previous chapter presented the Classis of Albany struggling to take its place in revivalist America, becoming an uneasy member of the club. Will it in turn find its place in the Protestant empire? It will eventually become an American church, a participant in the evangelical, democractic empire, but the process will not be smooth. With its roots in its particular Reformed polity, with a theology that does not lend itself to the empire, and with the arrival of immigrants in mid-century amalgamation into the American mainstream will prove neither quick nor easy.

Denominationalism

The rise of the empire was signaled by the appearance of the "denomination" on the American religious landscape. It needs to be made clear that "denomination" means something other than "church." Nor does it mean precisely those Protestant Christians who hold to a particular creed (or lack thereof) or are bound by a particular polity. Marty calls "denomination" a "studiously neutral term, a 'nothing' or noncommital word."[2] The Reformed had been a "church" in its connection to the Classis of Amsterdam prior to 1771, and had gathered in its synod since then. It wasn't, however, until the 1830s that the Reformed church began to become something like a denomination, an entity that could exist alongside other denominations and that began to take on a conscious structure of its own.

This was to happen as various boards of the church came into existence. As noted in chapter 2, subsquent to its experiment in mission by assigning the Classis of Albany as its Standing Committee on Mission, the General Synod relocated its commiteee to direct missions southward to New York City in 1818. Thus began a period of activity that would culminate in 1831 with the establishment of the Board of Missions (domestic missions). In 1832, the General Synod established the Board of Foreign Missions. Other boards were to follow: the Widow's Fund in 1837 and the Board of Publication in 1854.[3] The boards provided the beginnings of a "denominational" structure, a nascent bureaucracy, if you will, vis a vis the structured polity of assemblies: synods-classes-consistories.

While these boards made it possible for the denomination to "exist" between meetings of the General Synod, by themselves they were gatherings of people who acted "in committee." A further wrinkle was added with the hiring of "agents." The agent could and did work on behalf of the synod. While the synod had employed an agent before, the 1832 report of the Board of Missions advocated the use of an agent. However, its report recognized that this was to be a new turn in the old polity. The proposed general agent is

...a new office, unknown to the Constitution, it seems, like the office of deacon, to take its rise from circumstances. It is not an office of the Constitution of the Church of Christ as he gave it, nor do we pretend that it is a part of the "pattern exhibited"—there is no ordination to it, nor is it viewed as a standing department in his house, nor is it any thing more than a means of concentrating, in one person, the acts of the whole company of ministers, and prosecuting a given object by a system of operations.[4]

From that point on the Classis of Albany began to interact with the General Synod through the boards of the church, rather than directly. The new relationships can be seen primarily in matters of finance, specifically in the matter of collecting money to support denominational missions. The question to be answered was how that support would be raised.

This study has continually noted (and perhaps belabored) that the Reformed church was not about to accept a congregational polity. In fact, there was no question that the General Synod could assess the various classes for the expenses of the synod. The classes, in turn, could only devise means for distributing the costs among their constituent congregations. For example, in 1830, the Classis of Albany discovered that it owed the General Synod for its copies of the synod's minutes. The classis simply voted that each church pay one dollar toward the purchase of the minutes.[5] In 1850, the synod assessed the classis $350 as its portion of the repayment of a debt of the General Synod. The classis in turn apportioned the cost among its churches, assigning the most to the church of Albany at $100 and the least to the churches of Second Berne and Knox at one dollar per church.[6]

Matters were handled quite differently when it came to the cause of mission. Albany Classis never questioned the validity of the goals of the boards, and at times it supported them vigorously. However, it supported the boards through voluntary collections from the local congregations. Thus, in 1838, not long after the establishment of the board system, the classis resolved that

it be earnestly recommended to the Pastors & Consistories within this Classis to consider the vital importance of effectually sustaining the boards of Education & Missions in our church: & that (since the business of agencies for these objects is left by Genl. Synod to the Classes), they be urged to attend to the subject, each within his own charge & make collections, for the Education board on some Sabbath in Oct. & for the two missionary boards on some Sabbaths in Decr. & Feby.[7]

In this action it is important to note first that the classis clearly and explicitly retained to itself the task of raising funds, or better, soliciting benevolent contributions. Neither the General Synod nor its boards possessed the authority to approach the congregations on their own. Second, neither did Albany Classis itself impose an assessment on the churches. It simply urged a system of annual collections for the task. This proved to be a less than satisfactory solution.

The General Synod approached the classes through a different strategy when it established a building fund in 1854 to raise

$25,000 for the erection of church buildings. This time the synod
wanted each classis to appoint a team of two ministers and one
elder to solicit contributions from churches and individuals.
Albany Classis had little difficulty with the goal; it "earnestly
urged" the synod's goal upon the churches. But it added that once
a congregation had made its annual collection, it was not to be
visited again for the same purpose.[8] Just so the classis stood
between the congregations and the denomination, both urging the
churches to loyalty to the church and protecting the congregations
from unwanted intrusion.

Still, it was not an easy task that the classis urged on its
ministers. The necessity to meet the demands of the boards
became a constant plea and the classis continued to search for
better methods to help the congregations in their giving. In 1856
the classis promoted what it called the "Scriptural standard of
systematic benevolence." To encourage the churches in a united
task, the classis required that consistories report to the spring
session of classis what they had accomplished in the year past and
to add any suggestions or successes that might encourage other
churches in the classis.[9]

It was not always easy. The General Synod had leveled
assessments on the classis previously. It had long been
established that the classis determined the proportion that each
church was expected to pay. In 1861, as war loomed in the life of
the nation, several churches in Albany Classis simply refused to
pay their portion of the assessment (or "tax," as it is called in one
of the rate lists in its minutes). In turn the classis commented that
"some of our best churches have declined to pay their
assessment...& it is considered too great a burden for our weak
churches," and acted to decline to pay its assessment after 1861.
The classis overtured the General Synod either to reduce its
expenses or increase its "permanent funds" as would secure a
sufficient income for the synod's purpose.[10] The synod's
"purpose" was to raise money for a "contingency fund" to help
raise the salaries of the professors at the theological seminary.
While there is no record of this overture having reached the 1861
synod, the synod commented on two similar overtures in 1862.
The Committee on the Professorate simply could find no other
way to raise the money equitably and could do little more than

suggest that instead of the General Synod determining the amount to be assessed to each classis, it would devolve the task to the particular synods: New York would pay two-thirds, Albany one-third, while Chicago, a new and weaker synod, would be exempt.[11] About this time, in the early 1860s, Albany Classis began to report approaches made to it from secretaries and agents of the various boards. The needs of the boards will take up more and more of the classis's time and energy. At its spring meeting of 1862, the classis received urgent appeals from the Board of Foreign Mission, the Sunday School Board, the Board of Education, and the Board of the Corporation. The only boards it didn't hear from were from the Widow's Fund and Domestic Missions! In any case, the classis rescinded its action of the previous year not to pay its assessments.[12] By 1872, the classis's Committee on the Minutes of Synod could report, almost laconically, on the "usual & kindred recommendations in relation to our various Boards & exterior benevolent agencies...which are familiar to Ministers & Elders...."[13]

Not only did the requests become almost a standing item on the classis's agenda—the classis would yearly receive the communications and refer them to its overtures committee—but the amount demanded became ever greater. At its fall meeting in 1866, the classis received a letter from the secretary of the Board of Foreign Missions requesting that the classis increase its contribution by fifty percent over the previous year. The classis's reply reveals its desire to comply and the passion for mission it shared:

> Your Comtee. feel, that there should be something done immediately to relieve the embarassing condition of the Board. And that unless the churches afford the needed relief speedily our missions will prove a failure and we will be found guilty before God in denying the Bread of life to the perishing millions of India, China & Japan who are now crying for it.—God in his providence has made us the almoners of his bounty to those in the districts where our missions are situated, and woe be to us if we do not perform

the duty laid upon us. We will have to answer for the blood of souls. Your Comtee. recommend that extra efforts be put forth by each church in this classis to raise the amount desired, & more if possible so that we shall do our full proportion in spreading the glad tidings of salvation.[14]

Nor was that the end of the matter. Two months later the board circulated news of an immediate need for $46,000. The classis debated the matter for some time on the floor only to recommend to the churches that they take "such matters as they deem best suited to raise" their fair share of the full amount.[15]

This scenario repeated itself in the mid 1870s. In 1875, the Board of Foreign Missions requested $3,000 from the Classis of Albany. The classis in turn apportioned the request among its churches laying by far the greatest burden on First and Second churches of Albany—$1,600 and $500 respectively—while the rest of the classis was to bring offerings of between $10 to $225.[16] The amount remained about the same for a decade, until, in 1885, the board announced its "assessment" of the Albany Classis at $4000, an increase of $1,000. The classis didn't balk. It recognized that a greater effort was required, but encouraged the pastors to greater exhortations to their congregants for "more generous contributions."[17]

The relationship between the classis and the rising power of the denomination played itself out not only as the classis acted as a conduit for needed funds between the congregations and the various boards. From about mid-century on, the classis itself began to act through agents within the classis; its own members became representatives of various denominational causes. This was not always without resistance, and the classis could sometimes urge a stronger "central government" on the denomination. Thus, when, in 1852, the General Synod recommended that each classis appoint an agent from within its ranks to represent the Widow's Fund, the Classis of Albany refused. It judged that it would be "more equitable" for the General Synod to employ an agent. Then, in time-honored fashion, the classis recommended that each church receive a collection on behalf of the fund on the third Sunday of October.[18]

However, four years later, the Albany Classis was willing to go along with General Synod's recommendation that the classis appoint a colporteur (an agent to vend religious publications) on behalf of the Board of Publications. In fact, the classis was willing to go so far as to raise his salary and expenses from within the classis.[19] The classis has no record, however, of a person filling the position.

It wasn't until much later in the century, in 1883, that the General Synod requested, and the classis consented, to have its first "special agent" on behalf of missions present in the classis. The classis agreed and appointed the Rev. H. P. Craig of the Coeymans church as its first agent.[20] One need not look far to discover the reason for the appointment of the agent. The boards had struggled constantly to raise sufficient funds. In fact, in the early seventies, both the Board of Domestic Missions and the Board of Foreign Missions had complained about the method of raising money through designated collections. The classis had two collections annually for foreign missions and one for Domestic Missions. One peril of this method was observed by the Board of Domestic Missions. The time for their collection was, the board noted plaintively, "so often interrupted by storms." The classis agreed and recommended that every church hold a monthly collection for both domestic and foreign missions.[21] Even this was not an adequate response to the continued demand for money, for by the 1890s the classis received requests for over $12,000 for domestic and foreign missions. The classis did not resist the need but instead judged that benevolent contributions could be increased through a "regular" giving to the boards. It therefore established a permanent committee on "Systemic Benevolence" to urge congregations to begin a new means of raising money.[22]

Despite its readiness to display independence from the denomination, the Albany Classis hardly understood itself as a champion of a "populist" resistance to a centralizing authority. The classis saw itself as fully a part of the church and urged its churches to understand themselves likewise. At each fall session, the classis heard an extensive report from its Committee on the Minutes of Synod. The classis went so far one year to "enjoin upon each pastor & consistory the duty of considering and responding promptly to these injunctions of Synod."[23] The classis most certainly was not in the business of enforcing the edicts of the

General Synod. Still, it joined its churches together into one church and functioned as that institution that mediated between the local congregation and what was becoming a denomination in the second half of the nineteenth century.

The other side of the classis's financial picture showed denominational money flowing in as well as out. The classis did not hesitate to apply to the various boards for assistance. The Board of Education assisted students for the ministry, and the classis continually applied for assistance for its candidates. The Board of Domestic Missions was in the business of aiding faltering churches and the classis request such. At one meeting (Spring, 1871), the classis applied for $100 from the Board of Education on behalf of Fourth, Albany's (the German church) parochial school. It also applied for $400 from the Board of Domestic Missions for the Holland church and $200 from the same board for the Westerlo church. However, the classis turned down a request from the Clarksville church and instead urged them to approach the consistory at Union to consider calling a minister together. Later that same year, Clarksville returned with a similar request. Union had called someone on their own. Again the classis turned down Clarksville's request "in consideration of the indebtedness of the Board." The classis was not unmindful of the financial state of the denomination.[24]

Missions

Martin Marty considers the rise in Protestantism's consciousness of world mission within the context of empire. "...just as the American chosen people were asking what were the uses of choseness, Protestantism was inspired with a desire to convert people, to spread its civilization, to expand and conquer."[25] Two milieux were open to the missionizing tendency of the newly ambitious Protestants: the American west and the rest of the world.

The Reformed church's impulse to mission pre-dated the rise of the evangelical empire. The mission to Canada followed the migrating Dutch Reformed; it did not have "a story to tell to the nations." But the Reformed did unite with its other Protestants in the rise of the boards of missions in the early nineteenth century. The continued efforts to put the need for mission before the congregations shows how central the concern for missions was to the classis. In fact, by the end of the century, the churches of Albany Classis would expend 22 percent of their contributions on denominational benevolent objects, and 31 percent of their contributions on all benevolences.

The classis would have a personal stake in the evangelical cause of mission. On April 8, 1838, the classis ordained William J. Pohlman as a missionary at the North Church (First) in Albany. He was to become a missionary first in Borneo and later in Amoy. The classis would receive regular reports from overseas from him and would pause in their sessions to pray for him and his mission. Tragedy struck in 1848, when on returning from Hong Kong to Amoy, his ship was wrecked and he was lost, "the first instance of death by shipwreck of any of the missionaries of the American Board," according to Corwin.[26]

It is instructive, however, to see just how the Reformed church prosecuted the missionary task. Individual congregations did not send missionaries, but rather the boards themselves. For that matter, while the congregations collected contributions for mission support, it was the classis that acted as the go-between. The boards did not approach congregations except through the various classes.

In one instance, however, the Albany Classis tried sending its own missionary. Simon V. E. Westfall had been a pastor at the Union and Salem congregations when the classis sent him as a "missionary to the Western states" in 1847. He was to select his place of ministry "under the sanction of this Classis." For his assistance, the classis agreed to pay $100 for his outfit and an annual salary of $300. The following year, Westfall reported himself in Illinois. The classis informed him that Pekin was the best place for his new ministry. But the classis then transfered Westfall to the Classis of Illinois and transferred the mission to the Board of Domestic Missions. The classis was not about to enter the business of directing missions, at least not at that distance. Given its experience thirty years earlier in Canada, one can fairly assume that the classis knew that it could not undertake an active role in supporting a mission. That was not the last the classis heard of Westfall, however. The classis had never had an easy time paying him. In 1850, he wrote to report that his salary had been delayed and he was in dire straits. He was not pleased that his mission had been tranferred to the Board of Domestic Missions. The classis remained firm. It had sent him its share of the money. The best it could do was to call the matter to the attention of the Executive Committee of the Board of Domestic Missions.[27]

The cause of missions was not only urged on the congregations for increased contributions, but the classis furthered the missionary task in two other ways. First, a series of "missionary conventions" began by the early 1870s. On September 17, 1872, the classis "complied with" the calling of a missionary convention and set one at First Church in Albany on September 25 at 3:00 p.m. and 7:30 p.m., eight days later. Evidently it could be organized in a very short time![28] Eighteen years later, a special committee of the classis on Foreign and Domestic Mission Apportionments recomended not only that each church hold a missionary convention in order to raise money for mission, but that every Sunday school do the same![29]

At the same time a parallel effort to the work of the Board of Foreign Missions was taking place with the Women's Board of Foreign Missions. In 1881, the classis appointed two women, Mrs. Mary Pryn and Miss Emily Sumner, to cooperate with the women's board to raise an "earnest missionary spirit" in the churches and to raise funds to maintain missions "in foreign lands."[30]

Church Extension

As the Dutch church slowly joined the empire, it enjoyed a modest growth in the number of its churches. In the case of the Albany Classis, this happened through "church extension." In fact, by the mid 1870s the classis was to establish its first standing committee on Church Extension. The early middle to late nineteenth century was to witness the accession of a number of churches to the classis, most of which persist into the present. The new churches were not, however, the product of the period of revival in the American religious world, however the Reformed might welcome the new revivals. This is due in large part to the way in which congregations came into being.

The Constitution of the Reformed church in its various incarnations had very little to say about how congregations were to be organized. The church order of Dort, Article 38, required that no new consistory could be constituted "without the advice and concurrence of the Classis." This requirement was to be repeated through the revisions of the Constitution. The Explanatory Articles devolved on the classes the power of "forming new congregations, and determining the boundaries, where contested between congregations already formed" and "the continuing combinations, or the dissolution or change of the same, as may be requested by the people, or be judged necessary among the respective congregations" (Art. 39).

How did Albany Classis go about forming congregations? In the beginning, at least, it looked as though it didn't! It received congregations by supervising the election of a consistory. Records from 1793 show that the classis had organized several congregations that year: Beesick, Painston's Kill, Wynant's Kill, Mayfield, and Coeymans.[31] But more instructive is the case at Nisquethaw (Onesquethaw).

Several people living in the northwest part of the town of Bethlehem (not far from the city of Albany) approached the classis in April, 1802, to petition it for the formation of a new congregation. The classis responded with a committee! The committee reported five months later that it was inexpedient to proceed. Some of the petitioners lived within the bounds of the congregation pastored by Herman Van Huysen (either the Jerusalem or the Salem congregations). Instead, the committee urged that "attempts should be made" in the vicinity of Manhattan-Hook.[32] This was not an instance of a classis searching out a field where a congregation might be formed. In fact, there is no evidence that any "attempts" where made at Manhattan-Hook. Ironically, a Presbyterian church in Onesquethaw was to be dismissed from the Presbytery of Albany to unite with the classis in 1839.[33] One wonders if the potential congregants hadn't gone ahead and organized their church anyway. In any case, a church was well established by the 1830s.

The pattern of petitioning the classis, to have the classis then supervise the election of a consistory, was to repeat itself in the churches at Union (1809); Gibbonsville and West Glenville (1814); Second, Albany (1815); Rotterdam Junction (1818); and Princetown (1821). The Princetown church provided an interesting interaction with the General Synod. While the classis organized the church, the General Synod's Committee on Missions reported in 1822 that a Mr. Jared Downing had accepted a mission in Princetown. The committee went on to state that it had resolved that Mr. Downing was to "be considered under their employ" throughout the term of his employment.[34]

The same theme plays in the organization of the Second Church of Coxsackie. A group of people approached the classis to form a church in Coxsackie Landing since they were too far from the old village of Coxsackie to allow easy access to a church. Furthermore, the Baptists, the Methodists, and the Episcopalians were making major inroads into the Dutch flock. This was church extension as a defense![35]

A variation on the theme occurred in Albany in 1834 in the organization of the Third Church of that city. In this case, it was a pastor of the classis, Isaac Ferris, pastor of Second, Albany, who requested permission to form a third Dutch church in Albany and thus became the agent of a new congregation. Still, the classis did not take the initiative but acted only to grant Ferris the permission he required. Later (in 1835), the classis received a petition from a number of potential congregants and received Third into the classis.[36]

The classis gathered in September of 1842 to take action on two churches that were to enter the classis. First, it was to receive the Knox congregation which had been established as a Presbyterian congregation. The second case shows the classis in a more active mode. The classis itself decided to attempt to start a church in Troy. In this case, it was willing to put some money into the project. It pledged itself to raise $250 for this purpose in the year ahead, and would apply to the Board of Domestic Missions to appoint someone to work in Troy for $300 per year.[37]

The Second Church of Bethlehem (now Delmar) originated in yet another variation on the theme. Again, the classis took little active part in the first move to organize. Instead, several members of the Union church desired to divide the parish of Union into a western and an eastern section. This necessitated not only the presence of the classis to certify the election of a consistory, but involved the classis in the legal division of the assets of the Union congregation. The petition for a new congregation was received and granted in January, 1848.[38]

In the 1840s the classis had sent a minister into the Clarksville area to form a new congregation. By the time the church got around to applying for recognition and reception into the classis in 1854, it had already erected a building.[39] However, six months later, Clarksville was in trouble. It could not repay its debt on the building, and the classis had to request aid for the Clarksville congregation from its churches.[40] Relief was not forthcoming, and two years later, Clarksville again approached the classis requesting relief from its debt. The classis had few answers. Instead, the trouble provoked a long discussion on the effects of long vacancies on some of the churches of the classis. The classis's answer was to urge the uniting of several congregations for the calling of ministers. It urged Clarksville to join with the Salem and the Onesquethaw churches to call a pastor.[41] The classis's concerns over a church at Onesquethaw in 1802 had proven prophetic.

Greater activity in the development of new churches in Albany began in the 1850s. The more interesting cases have to do with new German and Dutch immigrants. But first to be noted is an aborted attempt by Third Church to beget a new church in Albany, the so-called "Dudley Church." Third had for some time been considering moving the church westward, "up the hill" in the city. The consistory had unanimously resolved to relocate. The congregation was not in full agreement. However, the pastor, Alexander Dickson, was ready to move. In January, 1860, the classis dissolved the relation between Dickson and Third Church. The minutes of that classis meeting note that a "meeting was held about this time, at which leave was granted to Br. Dickson to form a church to be located in the western portions of the city." About two-fifths of the congregation of Third applied for letters of dismissal to join Dickson in the new church. They chose a building site on Lancaster Street, near Swan. The new building was to cost $30,000; a Mrs. Dudley had already contributed half that amount.[42] By April, Dickson reported to the classis that he had organized a "Dudley Reformed Protestant Dutch Church."

The classis received the church. A year and a half later, in September, 1861, the classis dissolved the relationship between Dickson and the Dudley church, and by April, 1862, the classis reported that the church "has met with great reverses...suffered pecuniary embarassments, & is likely to have its new & beautiful church edifice sold, & the church dissolved." Within a year, the classis reported that the church had indeed been dissolved and sold.[43]

More interesting, and more successful, if a bit stormy, was the beginning of the Holland church in Albany. In September, 1846, I.N. Wyckoff, pastor of Albany's Second Church, brought letters to the classis "belonging to the persecuted dissenters from the national church [of the Netherlands] & begging the sympathy & aid of the R. Dutch Churches in N. America." The classis resolved that "this Classis is deeply impressed with the account of the difficulty of our evangelical brethren in Holland & would recommend to the churches of the Classis to take such action in the premises as their sympathy & love for the persecuted brethren may suggest & their own pecuniary ability may warrant."[44]

At the following stated meeting of the classis (April, 1847), Wyckhoff presented a twenty-three-year-old man from among the Dutch immigrants as a potential candidate for ministry. Wyckhoff had spoken to eighty or ninety of the immigrants, who reported themselves pleased with the young man, Mannes Mensink, and his preaching. Mensink had no money, but Wyckhoff thought that he might be useful, especially since Wyckhoff anticipated a much larger emigration from Holland to the United States. The classis agreed and recommended Mensink to the Board of Education of the General Synod. The classis hoped that although Mensink was not a graduate of an American college, he could by some means study theology so that he might become a preacher to the new immigrants.[45]

The minutes of the same meeting of the classis mention that between thirty and sixty immigrant Dutch were involved in Second, Albany's sabbath school. These were people who had fled "the oppression of the national church & the govt. of Holland." They had landed in Albany and found there that the doctrines on behalf of which they had fled the Netherlands were the very ones held as orthodox "by our church, at the present day" as the classis was to put it.[46]

The new Dutch had already been worshiping in Albany. The 1848 meeting of the classis reported that an A.B. Veenhuysen had been preaching to the Dutch in Albany. He applied to be received by the classis. On investigation, the classis discovered that he had studied classics and theology for seven years in Geneva, from there to become a professor of Sacred Languages and Literature in the Secession church in the Netherlands. He had never been "in the usual manner licensed," but had preached as "opportunity in providence demanded." The classis received him and began to take steps to license him.[47]

Four years later, in September, 1852, the classis received a document from a group of Dutch immigrants purporting to be a set of regulations for a church. The classis noted several differences from the polity of the Reformed Dutch church, including the admission of women to vote, the lack of elders, and the employment of a "helper" to manage the church. However, the classis reserved judgment on the rules until such time as the group was to become a church and apply for admission to the classis.[48]

The church made that application in 1853, but the classis still delayed. The minutes of classis mention certain "difficulties" but do not specify the nature of the trouble.[49] That there were indeed difficulties is clear from a report to the classis later that year and the withdrawal of the petition by the congregation.[50]

It wasn't until September, 1859, that about sixty Dutch immigrants applied to be admitted to the classis. The congregation reported that it had selected elders and deacons. The classis appointed a committee to organize the church and resolved that the church should raise no less than $300 for the calling of a minister.[51]

Within eight years, however, the classis was to take note of serious problems in the Holland church. In January, 1869, a classis committee reported to the full body (over two and a half years after its appointment!). It found serious division in the church over what it called "gross irregularities" on the part of those chosen "or claim to be chosen" as consistory. One elder admitted, for example, that he was not even a member of that church but was a suspended member of another congregation.

Furthermore, the classis discovered from the consistory minutes that the consistory had regularly ignored the constitution, acting more according to congregational than presbyterial polity. For example, congregational meetings were called to dismiss members and to act in matters of discipline. The classis concluded that the consistory had forfeited all right to be recognized. The classis then declared all discipline enacted by the church for the past two years null and void. The classis further directed that the congregation elect a new consistory, as though it were a new congregation.[52]

All ended well, however. By 1895, the Holland church enjoyed sufficient strength to boast that it expected to be self-sustaining for the first time within the following year.[53] The larger church had supported the congregation for nearly forty years.

The organization of the German church (Fourth) was less stormy. This was not the first appearance of Germans in Albany. There had been a German church under Reformed auspices briefly in the 1770s. It had been disbanded and its property sold by 1794.[54] In the early nineteenth century, the classis had detailed John Bassett to ask a committee of the General Synod to confer with the Coetus of Pennsylvania for the purpose of finding preachers who could speak both German and English to supply the needs of Germans in the Albany area.[55]

In 1855, the classis received a petition from fifty Germans living in the south side of Albany for the organization of a new church. The church had been started as a mission project of the Albany Tract and Mission Society. However,

> it was necessary to give it a Protestant Reformed basis. After preaching the Gospel for three month to about 25 hearers in the average, a Series of inquiry meetings were held, to find out the truely regenerated Christians, by which occasions it pleased God to convert a youth and a catholic woman.[56]

Six months later, the classis agreed.[57] Within three years, the report on the state of religion noted that the Albany churches had purchased a building for the "German missionary church."[58] The classis wasn't the only organization involved with this church. The Tract and Missionary Society of Albany applied to the classis for financial help in paying the pastor of the German church. The classis declined; it simply didn't have the money. But, in by now regular practice, the classis allowed the pastor of the German church to put his case before the churches of the classis.[59]

However, the church labored under the burden that its building was owned jointly by First and Second churches. Thus, when Fourth reported itself in financial trouble in 1876, the classis recommended to the trustees of First and Second churches that they transfer the property to Fourth "with all suitable restrictions." It wasn't until April, 1890, that the classis could report that First and Second had agreed.[60]

Again, the story had a happy ending. Just after the turn of the twentieth century, the Germans announced that their church hoped to become self-supporting. In fact, they could report that they now held two English language services a month.[61]

By 1868, the classis was to take greater initiative in the establishment of new churches. It appointed a committee of three pastors—H.M. Voorhees of Bethlehem, J. Elmendorf of Second, Albany, and A.C. Millspaugh of Jerusalem—and two elders—Gilbert Wemple of Bethlehem and C. H. De Forest—to investigate the establishment of a new church in the area served by the Bethlehem church "adjacent to the river." Two years later, Voorhees reported that a William Bogardus had been hired as a missionary. Classis liked what it heard and encouraged the work, adding J. L. Pearse of the Second, Bethlehem, church to the committee.[62] In the event, no congregation was founded.

Then, in September, 1872, the classis appointed its first Standing Committee on Church Extension.[63] There is little evidence of active work, however, until 1885, when the classis appointed a special committee to investigate the possibility of erecting a chapel in Voorheeseville to operate in connection with the New Salem church.[64] Little appears to have come of the effort. Indeed, little appears to have occurred at the initiative of classis.

It is true that the classis appointed a committee to form a church in West Albany (Sixth) in 1897. However, the church reported itself ready within three months with fifteen people who had their membership certificates from other churches at the ready. This was hardly time for extended investigation.[65] Two years later, the Rev. David Williams addressed the classis about his work at Normanskill. The classis appointed a committee to investigate further, but little happened.[66]

The classis had seen growth in the number of its churches. However, in most successful instances, it had been less active than reactive. When its turn came to taking the initiative to establish churches, the classis could claim little success.

Ecumenics

If growth in the number of its churches shows the classis joining the great Protestant empire, an examination of its ecumenical posture also displays the classis as a conscious participant in the culture of American Protestantism. The difficulties in pursuing an ecumenical agenda also revealed by the end of the century that the Reformed were not ready to become full members of a united American church.

From early on, the classis had looked favorably on relations with other denominations. Already in 1789, the General Synod had wrestled with how this Dutch church was to relate to other Protestant churches who had established themselves in the new country. The question cut most sharply in the case of the Presbyterians. Here was a church with an almost identical polity and similar confessional foundation. The synod requested the opinion of its various classes. Albany responded by leaving the matter to the synod. However, it desired that "some regulation be made with respect to members who pass over from one denomination to another, that in such case there be no complusion, but the same take place in mutual confidence.[67]

At the beginning of the century Albany emitted further signals of an ecumenical spirit. John Johnson of the Albany church preached the first fourth of July sermon published in Albany in 1805. At this time the city, while having been under British influence for well over a century, was largely led by the Dutch burghers. Johnson urged, however, that the Dutch not resist efforts to dissolve their homogeneity. Instead the common council, under the influence of the Dutch, was to view the establishment of new churches as a desirable way of promoting the common religious bonds of a diverse population.[68]

In fact, still early in the century, the General Synod approached the synod of the Associate Reformed church, a Reformed body of Scottish Covenanters that confessed the Westminster as the foundation of their faith, with an eye to union. The General Synod noted that the two churches were in "cordial agreement on doctrines" with but "minor differences." The Classis of Albany agreed unanimously. It was not to be. The Presbyterian body declined.[69]

One problem the classis had in its ecumenical relationships had continued to puzzle it. What was it do to with ministers who hoped to enter Reformed pulpits from outside its polity? While the classis struggled with the polity issue, and while it hesitated at times, it did receive ministers from other denominations. This was easiest, of course, with Presbyterians; they shared both polity and theology. But the classis could and did receive a Baptist or a Congregationalist here and there, provided, of course, that they be properly examined by the classis.

At times, the classis had to strain logic to the breaking point to accomplish the deed. This was so in the case of one Benjamin Romaine. He had been ordained by a council of Congregational ministers, and in April of 1858, he applied for admission to the classis. Admission posed a problem; he was not connected to an association, a body the classis judged to be somewhat equivalent to a classis. He had, however, been preaching within the classis. In fact, he was a member of a church in the classis! What was the classis to do? The classis reasoned that Congregational polity was not uniform anyway. Since Romaine was working in a church in the classis at the time, since he was well known to the members of the classis, and since the Constitution didn't describe how classes were to go about receiving members from other churches, the classis argued that it could examine Romaine.

Still, problems remained. There was no one present who could act as a deputatus from the synod. The classis undertook a new bout of reasoning and decided that the term "candidate" was meant to apply to people who apply for licensure and ordination, not to those who had been ordained and now seek admission to another body. The classis could proceed to admit Romaine.[70]

Nor did the classis hesitate unduly in considering union with one of the other Reformed bodies in the United States, the German Reformed church. In April, 1844, the classis approved the plan of the General Synod for union with the German church. The synod's plan culminated a long and cordial correspondence between the Dutch and the German churches. The plan did not envision full organic union, but instead initiated a triennial convention of thirty-six elders and ministers, one-third Dutch and two-thirds German. The convention was to have no legislative or judicial power but was to promote cooperation, especially as the two synods looked to their mission to the west. Furthermore, since the German church was finding it difficult to fill its pulpits, the Dutch agreed to urge its ministerial students to look to possible service among the Germans. The plan was accepted and one convention was held. Among the delegates from the Dutch side were Isaac Ferris, formerly of Second, Albany, and John Ludlow, formerly of First, Albany. However, the effort proved to be a failure as the friendship fell victim to the controversy and the misunderstandings of what came to be called "Mercersburg theology."[71]

The question of union with the Germans did not disappear. However, when it arose later in the century, the classis began to look elsewhere for union. In 1887, the classis noted that since union with the German church was again in the air, why not pursue union with other bodies holding a similar doctrine and polity? Just so, the classis overtured the General Synod to adopt a plan for union between the Reformed church and the Presbyterian Church in the United States of America. Albany's neighboring classis, Schenectady, presented a similar overture to the same General Synod.

The synod responded quickly and sharply. It had also received an overture from the Synod of Chicago, "representing six classes," that judged that "any agitation of organic union with any other denomination" is "unwise and detrimental to our Church work." The General Synod, doing some quick and easy arithmetic, discovered that with six classes opposed to union and only two requesting it, that "it would only be detrimental to our peace, unity and prosperity" to pursue union, and furthermore "it is the duty of the Reformed Church...not to agitate and probably disrupt itself with vain questions...."[72]

Still, by the 1890s the question of union with the German church returned. The 1891 General Synod had proposed a plan for a "Federal Synod of the Reformed Churches." The plan allowed each denomination to remain intact, complete with its own

General Synod. The federated synod would have as its main task mission, new educational enterprises, and a general superintendance of the Sunday schools. It could recommend action to the respective General Synods, but it would not interfere with the "creed, cultus or government" of either church.[73]

This time, the Classis of Albany voted not to approve the General Synod's plan. Why not? The report to the General Synod of 1892 gives us some clues. Remarkably, twenty-four of the thirty-three classes voted in favor of the union. Some hesitated and proposed changes. Others desired a broader plan, desiring a similar union with all churches holding the presbyterial polity.[74] Given Albany's proposal for union just five years earlier, one suspects that the latter is what the classis had in mind in its reservation.

The vote of the classes was sufficient to proceed to union with the German body. All that was needed was a declarative vote by the General Synod. The synod voted to delay action. By the following year the vote reversed, and of the thirty-four classes voting, eighteen voted against union. Something happened. And what happened can shed light on the Reformed church's wider attempt to join the empire.

The main opposition to union came from the churches in the west. These churches emerged from the mid-ninteenth century immigration from the Netherlands. New to this country, they struggled to maintain their identity in a strange land. They could not yet have experienced the process of Americanization that two centuries of life had nurtured in the rest of the church. Thus, a campaign, centered at Western Seminary, mounted agitation against union especially on the pages of the *Christian Intelligencer*, the denominational paper. Opponents charged in the main that union brought with it the possibility of heresy and heterodoxy. Their arguments did not carry the day in the rest of the church. However, the larger church did harbor a real concern that a schism of the churches of the west might result if the union were to be approved.[75] So, out of deference to its recent, immigrant population, the General Synod declined the opportunity for union.

Immigration

The immigrant experience was not strange to the Classis of Albany. It had a small but vital connection with the nineteenth-century Dutch who found their way to this country. The Holland Church in Albany had emerged from the arrival of Dutch immigrants, refugees from ecclesiastical tensions in the Netherlands. These immigrants were happy to find the "old faith" still maintained in the new world. Their presence reminded the Dutch church of its peculiar origin.

The classis also looked west and encouraged the growth of the church in Michigan. This was not a missionary enterprise, at least not in the sense that the church entered an area to convert the residents to a new faith. These were coreligionists who entered this country and settled on the shores of Lake Michigan. As early as 1840, Albany Classis took note of the new population and requested of the Particular Synod of Albany that it form a new classis in Michigan, or any other territory, as soon as the requisite number of ministers and churches were to be found.[76]

Likewise, within a couple generations, the classis was looking with favor upon a new college in the West. In 1865, the classis had on its agenda a request from Philip Phelps, an Albanian who would become president of the new Hope College in 1866. Phelps had graduated from Union College and New Brunswick and had been licensed by the classis. He requested and the classis agreed to endeavor to raise $1,000 from the churches of the classis to establish a scholarship at the school on behalf of the classis.[77]

Identity—Theology and Liturgy

While the immigrant experience reminded the church of its Reformed identity, the classis was also concerned to maintain its sense of who it was in contradistinction to the "empire." This is not to argue too strongly that the immigrants caused a retrogression from a more enculturated religious expression. The immigrants may simply have accentuated differences that already existed.

The classis had its eye on its theology as, for example, it constantly refers itself to the preaching and teaching of the

Heidelberg Catechism. It kept reminding itself, its ministers, and its churches that the catechism stood at the center of its life. One gets the sense, however, that in actual practice, the catechism was honored more in word than in actual preaching and teaching. The continuing reminders suggest that preachers found it difficult or inconvenient to comply with the regulation that they preach regularly on the catechism. One report on the state of religion laments that the preaching on the catechism was "still lightly regarded."[78] A few years later, the classis reported again that only one preacher (I.N. Wyckoff) had preached in "full compliance" on the catechism. "Some of the Brn. had preached one or more lectures—others had preached the doctrine, but not from the catechism."[79] Still even when not preaching on the catechism, the classis was fully aware that in some way the catechism made this Dutch church unique.

The classis was fully aware of its "Reformed" identity when it measured itself against "newer" doctrines, much as they saw present among the Methodists. In 1848, the classis urged that Dr. Wyckoff publish his two sermons on "The Cause, Evil, & Remedy of a Migratory Ministry."[80] This is leveled at the Methodists. By the early 1870s, the Fourth Church of Albany reported that ten of their members left for "another fold." The classis counseled the distraught church not to be concerned: "...if they can be more useful & more happy among the Methodists they should have been dismissed with the Benediction...if our heavy seige guns—the Canons of Dort—are too hard for some of our friends to handle they may join the flying artillery if they please."[81]

The classis was no more "liberal" when it came to a move to change the name of the Reformed church. The 1853 General Synod proposed that the church change its name by dropping the word "Dutch" from its title. The synod agreed that the term was accurate in its historical reference, but that it impeded the growth of the church. Only one church in the classis, First of Albany, agreed with the recommended change. Evidently, most of the Reformed church agreed with the majority of the classis.[82] It was not until 1867 that the denomination finally changed its name to "The Reformed Church in America." By that time, the classis agreed.[83]

Likewise, the classis resisted changes in the liturgical forms of the church. The General Synod began work in 1853 to revise the liturgy. When the classis finally got to reviewing the work of the synod, it concluded that most of the changes were too unimportant to warrant a full revision of the liturgy. The time had "not yet come" to be able to rewrite the liturgy with "entire unanimity & good feeling." The changes were but a "few verbal alterations." As it happened, very little was changed except in the "Exposition" or the "Meaning of the Sacrament" of Baptism, where the classis agreed with the synod that "he was innocently condemned" should read "he, although innocent, was condemned." Corwin comments laconically: "Thus ended the first attempt, after five years of labor, to revise the Liturgy. The only result was the correction of a single grammatical error."[84]

Throughout the rest of the century, the classis resisted proposed changes in liturgical practice. For example, the classis did not much like a new marriage form proposed by the General Synod in 1875, instead resolving "that the old form be allowed to stand."[85]

Social Concerns

The concerns of the Protestant empire (northern division) turned throughout the century on temperance, sabbath keeping, abolition of slavery, and perhaps sufferage. The classis had always been concerned about Sabbath keeping and temperance. What of the other concerns of the empire? After all, it was at the middle of this century that war broke out between the States.

There is no evidence of concern for the cause of slavery from the classis as a body. Indeed, throughout the period of the Civil War, one finds little mention of the war at all. Soon after its outbreak in 1861, the classis echoed the concern of the General Synod on the political situation. The synod fundamentally supported the government's quest for unity, remembering the Dutch experience of war three centuries previous! But the classis was "grieved at the needless violation of the sabbath by our govt. or our armies." Furthermore, the classis commended the actions of General McClellan on enforcing sabbath observance.[86] Slavery took a back seat to sabbath observance!

Otherwise, the classis limited itself to comments on the effect of the war on the life of its congregations, noting one time that the state of religion was in decline as a result of the "agitation" caused by the "southern rebellion," and the consequent drop in contributions. Yet another time the classis commented that the "differences of political opinion have made some trouble, & the rebellion has been generally injurious to the progress of religion."[87]

Otherwise, the classis showed little concern for social issues. Notable only by its exception is a minute in which the classis received a letter opposing polygamy in Utah. The classis agreed with the correspondant and requested its delegate to General Synod to use what influence he had to get General Synod to oppose the dangerous practice.[88]

The Classis of Albany came to the end of its first century, an American church but with its distinct identity intact and its polity firmly in place. It continued to struggle with its theological place and its liturgical forms, but it was a confident church, too. However, to see just how it understood itself in its own life, it will be necessary to review its internal life. It is to that task that this study now, if ever so briefly, turns.

V
An Evangelical Body

Even as the Classis of Albany was becoming a constituent of a denomination that took its place in America's Protestant culture, it still understood itself as a distinct body, a "classis." It met twice a year, spring and fall, in its "regular "sessions, but often was required to gather several times during the year to attend to such business as approving calls and dissolutions between pastors and congregations, examining students, and other business that could only be concluded by this local, trans-parochial body. Its concerns remained neither congregationally based nor nationally directed, notwithstanding the fact that as a "mediating institution" it drew the congregations from the danger of localism even as it allowed them to express their local concerns in a broader context. The classis tended to a life of its own. This chapter will show how the classis lived its peculiar life within the context of the mildly evangelical empire of the second half of the nineteenth century.

The culture will impact the life of the classis itself. The classis will reflect not only in its churches, but in its own common life, the hegemony of evangelicalism. And it will encourage its churches in the ways of the Protestant empire. Just how the classis found its way cannot be simply described for it engaged the ruling assumptions, perhaps without knowing consciously what it was about. It could not simply resist; nor did it appear to desire resistance. At the same time, it did not allow the churches and ministers to find their own way. It remained, explicitly, a classis, a structured way of being the church.

The Meeting

That the classis understood itself as a distinct body is evident from its concern for its own life. In a real sense, the classis could be said to "exist" only when it gathered as ministers and elders. It subsisted as a continuing institution, but without building and without what today would be called a "paid staff." Its president was elected from meeting to meeting, and while it remunerated a stated clerk, who often remained in office until he ceded the position, it took some time before the classis delegated any authority to committees that could carry on the work of the classis between sessions. This meant that most of the work of the classis took place at the time of the meeting.

This is not to say that the meetings were themselves particularly inviting. Even the clergy, whose primary ecclesiastical identity was found in the classis, were not always eager to attend. In fact, in 1855, at a stated session, only four clergy showed up, prompting the classis to act:

Whereas, this Classis consider it a solemn & imperative duty for the members & delegates of Classis to attend its meetings. And Whereas they have been grieved with the repeated absence of ministers & elders, & earnestly desire to correct this evil. Therefore Resolved, That the stated clerk notify delinquents that a formal excuse will be demanded of them—& that if any member be absent twice without excuse, he be considered under citation to appear at the next meeting & answer.[1]

The minister and elder are so firmly tied to the classis that they can be "cited" for failing to appear. Still, they felt themselves free enough not to attend. Here is evidence of a church that lives both congregationally in the spirit of the age, and still understands itself as a polity that refuses to be reduced to congregationalism. The tensions of Americanization express themselves in the attendance roster of the classis meeting!

In what almost seems a perverse example of compounding a bad situation, only a year later the classis announced to its members that, from henceforth, the delegates were to arrive expecting to spend two days in each stated session of the classis![2] The classis recognized that its meetings, while necessary, may not always have excited the interests of its participants, for within the year (1857) it voted to make its sessions "more interesting," especially to the local church where the classis happened to meet. A sermon was to be preached at the opening of the meeting, and in the evening of the first day, the classis would engage in devotional exercises that would include addresses and prayers.[3]

The classis, then, met not simply to conduct business; it became a society, a gathering not of the churches so much as of the leadership of the churches. Through its meetings the faith of the churches, and perhaps of the classis members themselves, could be strengthened. One detects here the evangelical temper of the age expressed in a peculiarly Reformed way. These were no local meetings, to which the leadership might be invited. This was the classis itself, the "company of pastors," to use Genevan language. It was in the gathered church officers that something like revival work would take place.

The two-day arrangement didn't last long. It returned, however, in the early 1880s. The classis altered its fall session this time, to expand from one to two days, "having in special view the promotion of an increased interest among us in the active work of the church, particularly its missionary & benevolent work." The classis proposed that in the afternoon of the first day, following "unfinished business" on the agenda, it would engage in a time of "prayer and conference" in anticipation of special services to follow in the evening. In the evening, the classis was to focus on such questions as:

How to promote the cooperation of all departments of the church?

How to make the prayer meeting to the fullest degree what it should be?

How to advance benevolence?

How to reach the different classes in the communities?

What are the obstacles in the way of evangelical work?

The tendencies of the times to be guarded against.[4]

Indeed, the classis followed through on this scheme. At its spring session in 1883, it announced that the topic for the fall session would be "What can be done to induce young men to enter the Gospel Ministry?" The following fall the question became "How shall we conduct the preaching or explaining of the

Catechism—whether by a short explanation on each Sabbath or by regular sermon on Stated Sabbaths." In 1885, the subject was once again the preaching of the Heidelberg Catechism.[5] The subjects proposed focused on the sort of questions that would be expected in a church in the "evangelical mainstream" of the later nineteenth century. The actual topics chosen, on the other hand, focused on concerns closer to the heart of Reformed preachers: on the recruitment and training of ministers for the churches and on the nettlesome problem of preaching the Catechism. The more evangelical churches needed to worry about neither.

This is not to say that the classis was somehow at the forefront of the consciousness of the churches—nor perhaps even of the pastors. One day, in fact, the classis showed up to meet in the First Church in Albany with nary a soul expecting the delegates' arrival. The minutes for the day report:

> In consequence of some oversight no preparation had been made for the meeting of the Classis in the 1st Ch. of Albany. The day was very cold & with no fire the room was unsuitable for the exercises of the Classis. After an hour's delay the meeting was commenced & Dr. Cornell requested that he be excused from preaching the usual sermon under the circumstances:—whereupon it was resolved that he be excused & the Sermon be omitted.[6]

The classis existed; it performed its (important) functions; but it remained in the background.

City and Country Churches

While it was the case that in a certain sense the classis only "existed" when meeting, the classis also knew itself as a confederation of churches. Just so, it understood itself as a collection of churches that ministered both in the "city" and in the "country." The city, of course, was Albany, which by the second half of the century had five Reformed churches. The country was the county (with the exception of the New Baltimore church, just over the border of the county in Greene County).

Indeed, the classis used the language of "city" and "country" to describe its constituent congregations. The annual reports from the consistories would often detail how the country churches could not meet for several weeks in the winter because of inclement weather. This fact made for financial hardships; if the church didn't meet, there was no collection. In one instance, the classis had to reprimand its country cousins for a rather easy-going approach to church life. On reviewing the consistorial records in 1867, the classis commented that "two or three" consistories did not report stated meetings. Thus the classis recommended "as far as possible the various Country Churches meet statedly at least four times a year."[7]

The relative strength in the city and country churches can be measured in the statistics over several years. In figures that remain roughly constant over the period in question, the five city churches held slightly more than fifty percent of the total number of communicants in the classis (the rest were distributed among the twelve country churches). The disparity in strength is the more striking, however, if one compares the giving of the city to the country churches. In benevolent giving, the city churches contributed 87.7 percent of the $8,921.03 given in 1860, and 88.6 percent of the $16,774.07 given in 1890 (with the First and Second churches of Albany contributing the lion's share of the city churches' giving). Similar, although slightly less significant, ratios are found in the contributions for congregational life. In 1860 the city churches contributed in total approximately three times what the country churches gave. The ratios remained constant through the century.[8]

One needs to be careful not to construe the classis's self-understanding of being a confederation of city and country churches as a devisive factor in the classis. In fact, the observer is impressed by how often ministers and elders from the city churches enter into active concern for their country counsins and vice versa. It does display, however, that the classis did understand itself as a trans-local reality that refused to be trapped into "natural" configurations.

Growth and Decline

As might be expected from a church participating in the evangelical spirit of its age, the classis kept an eager eye out for revivals and was ready to encourage the churches when they appeared. In 1858, for example, the annual Classical Report mentions "cheering revivals" in Albany, Salem, and Westerlo and adds that "Special Services have been held in all the churches with manifest benefit & a spirit of prayer has unusually prevailed."[9]

A decade later, in 1868, the classis was noticing signs of a true strengthening of its congregations. It warned that numbers could not tell the entire story, but noted, "The record in the column for conversions is one calculated to cheer & encourage every heart & stimulate to greater faith & more earnest effort for the future." In fact, the statistical table for the year reported that 184 persons had been received on confession.[10] By the following year, the classis was describing in detail the revivals in its churches. Of note is the report of the Bethlehem church. Its consistory related that the previous summer it had held prayer meetings but had found little interest. However, in January of 1869, several people began hold prayer meetings in homes, originally hosting four meetings per week. The results surprised them:

> The first meeting manifested that the Spirit of grace & supplication had been sent down with the continuance of the meetings—the interest increased until they became too strait in the houses & an extraordinary service was appointed in the church at wh. Eleven publicly declared themselves under conviction. A few meetings were held, two in a week for four weeks at wh. time the word of Salvation was preached—& at the close of the services—it was found that ninety-six had become inquirers after salvation & nearly all gave conclusive evidence that Jesus was more precious to their souls. At the communion in March 75 professed faith in Jesus Christ & have ever since manifested they follow no longer the way of the world.—Christians have been revived. Many family altars erected—Many Christians heretofore unused to pray in public have taken part together with those who have recently believed in Jesus Christ. Seven prayer meetings have been established in different parts of the congregation. As a

special feature a children's prayer meeting is held once a week at the parsonage & boys between the ages of eight and fifteen are active in prayer & are daily laboring for the conversion of their schoolmates.

And in fact, the classis reported that 302 persons had united with its churches through confession.[11]

Another decade later, the classis celebrated a season of revival in language that exults in "increasing evidence that his brooding tenderness & powers of grace are ever over & near & are never withheld from accesible hearts." Its State of Religion report notes a "commendable degree of spiritual life...taking form of an inward quickening of spiritual life & there births into the kingdom of God." In words that reflect nineteenth century American pietism, the classis took special note of events in Westerlo, where "a company of farmers, night after night coming to the house of God & pleading with deep earnestness for the descent of the Holy Spirit."[12]

Nor was this only a rural phenomenon. The following year, the classis reported that the churches in the "city" were enjoying a "Pentecostal blessing." First Church in Albany was reporting twelve to thirteen hundred folk were gathering in the "audience room" of First for a series of "morning meetings." "Hundreds have been brought to believe in the Lord Jesus Christ & multitudes have testified to the quickening influences they have experienced in the spiritual atmosphere that has filled the temple of God."[13]

The classis could not, however, report an always smooth and steady increase in souls entering the kingdom—or remaining in the church. Despite the fact that some of the smaller churches reported large gains in particular years, their relative size remained little changed over the longer stretch of years. And the classis but three years after the report of the large gatherings in Albany's First Church reflected a sense of discouragement in the churches, of "distraction." In 1879, the classis reported not only a loss of members, but more painfully had to record that the number received through confession of faith dropped by nearly 100: "...the times on which as ministers & elders in the chs. we are cast in more than one sense peculiarly hard times."[14] Three years later, in 1882, the classis again reported a shrinkage in its total membership of almost 200 (as well as a drop in contributions for congregational purposes of almost twenty percent), and remarked that "it does not require an exceedingly keen discrimination to observe that we are retrograding."[15]

In fact, it is in the period in question that the reports on the State of Religion show an increasing interest in statistics. Each year the committee charged with the report carefully took note of increases and declines, busily taking the temperature of piety in the numbers reported—even as the writers were quick to acknowledge that the numbers could not, of course, tell the entire story of spiritual growth and decline. Efficiency and results, modernist concerns par excellence, have found their way into the life of the classis.

Still, the classis remained active and alert in the cause of evangelism through the end of the century. In fact, the classis took the initiative when, in 1896, it appointed three members to act as a "Committee on Classical Evangelistic Visitation." Their task was to correspond with the various ministers as to speakers and dates, presumably for evangelistic meetings in the churches.[16]

Care for the Churches

As it had been from the beginning, the classis continued an active concern for the congregations in its care. This did not change with the rise in strength of the denomination or in the atmosphere of (sometimes overheated) revivals. Structurally, the classis continued its intention of visiting each consistory. In 1856, the classis noted that it "favored" visiting each church by committee and left it to each consistory to set the time for visitation and to invite the committee from classis to its meeting.[17] It is doubtful that this scheme worked very well, for eleven years later, in 1867, the classis outlined a project and scheduled teams of two ministers each to visit each consistory. Evidently that was accomplished, as many consistories reported to classis the following year that they had appreciated the visits of the teams from classis.[18]

Albany Classis kept a sharp eye on what was happening in its churches. In 1852, the classis grumbled at the Salem church over its ministerial arrangement. The church had employed Jasper

Middlemas as supply for their pulpit. The classis judged it "unconstitutional and irregular" for the church to continue such a supply arrangement indefinitely and instructed the church either to call Middlemas or the classis would require him to "retire from the supply." The church did get around to calling Middlemas—about a year later![19]

Likewise, the classis, unhappy with a continued vacancy, intervened in Westerlo. It "advised" the church to find itself a pastor to settle in residence. However, the classis added that it could do so only with the prospect of the "usual aid from the Board of Domestic Missions."[20]

At times it was the churches themselves who approached the classis. In 1864, the Union church asked the classis "what was to be done in their circumstances?" The classis could do little more than form a committee to visit the church and authorize the appointed force to apply to the Board of Missions for assistance (up to $300).[21]

At other times, the classis could be more direct. In one case, concerning the Jerusalem church, the classis instructed the Jersualem Consistory to rescind an action taken in relating to its "Sabbath School."[22] At still other times, the classis acted more indirectly. Its Committee on Church Visitation, for example, induced the classis to request of the pastors to preach on the duties of elders and deacons "in order to stir up consistories to a deeper interest in the active work of the church."[23]

The Ministers

The classis continued to concern itself not only that the pulpits of the churches be supplied with installed pastors, but that there be sufficient pastors to supply the pulpits. During the later half of the nineteenth century, new concerns about the ministry began to surface.

One such concern was with the state of the various pastors' salaries. Already in 1853, the classis entered conversation with itself that reflected a worry over the meager state of clergy compensation. "It is a fact," the classis reported, "that can no longer be disguised, that at the present high rate of living, the salaries of many brethren in the ministry are found inadequate to their competent support & that some of them in consequence of this inadequacy are trammeled & greatly burdened in their devotion to their proper labors & constrained to think of changing their field of labor, or even of abandoning the work of the ministry altogether...." The classis then urged the consistories to consider increasing the salaries of their pastors, "such as the respective circumstances of the respective pastors may demand."[24]

Whether the classis encouragement made any difference is not known. In 1863, the classis recorded the salaries offered by the various churches to their ministers (the table was used to formulate a "rate bill" for the churches). The list, at the very least, indicates the wide divergence of clerical compensation:

Albany	$3000	Westerlo	$450
2nd, Albany	1500	Jerusalem	500
3rd, Albany	300	Salem	450
4th, Albany		Union	200
Holland, Albany	300	Clarksville	100
Bethlehem	900	Onesquethaw	100
2nd, Bethlehem	800	2nd, Berne	1000
Coeymans	600		
New Baltimore	600.[25]		

How does this compare with individual income in mid-century? One measure is wages offered to workers on the Erie Canal. Top wages stood at $2.00 per day in 1850, or about $600 per year. In 1875, the average income measured in several cities in neighboring Massachusetts stood at $763 per year, with subsistence need measured at $427 per year.[26]

The problem did not go away, for by the end of the century, the classis again discussed with alarm the fact that some of its ministers were not paid regularly. However, the classis did little more than impress the obligation on the churches "by means of this report."[27]

In some sadder individual cases, the classis could do very little. In 1884, J.L. Zabriskie left the pastorate of the New Baltimore church for reasons of health. He asked the classis for permission to enter "any secular business" as a means of support. The classis sympathized with him in his physical disability, prayed for the restoration of his health and his return "to the labor of the church," and then granted his request. It is notable, however, that he had to request permission of the classis to enter "secular employment."[28]

But what in the late twentieth century has been misnamed clergy "firings" also began to occur. In several instances the classis approved the dissolution of a pastoral relation with no reason given, and the clergy with no call in hand. Two examples from 1891 suffice. The classis approved the dissolution of the relation between First, Bethlehem, and L. Dykstra, and then granted that Dykstra be "dismissed to such ecclesiastical body as he may designate." Likewise, the classis dissolved the relation between George Macardel and the New Salem church and ordered the Macardel be given a letter of dismission "to any other classis or body...when desired."[29]

In the concern of the classis for its ministers, the observer confronts the reality and the limit of classical authority. The classis was required to act, and it did act, not always to the liking of either minister or congregation. At the same time, it refused to do more than to recommend salary increases, and was apparently powerless, by the end of the century, to stop churches from dismissing their pastors.

VI
Turning Into a New Century (1893-1918)

In 1893, Chicagoans witnessed a colorful parade of Hindus, Moslems, Jews, Jains, Parsees, Buddhists, and Christians too, as delegates to the World's Parliament of Religions gathered for a sort of religious World's Fair. The fair heralded the dawn of a new era of peace between religions as the turn of the century promised an era of political peace. Neither was to be. But the Chicago gathering indicated a magnanimity among some, especially Protestant Christians, that issued from a sense of well-being. This was the turn into America's century, the era of manifest destiny, the rise of progressivism and the notion that with the tools of modernity to hand, humans could create a benevolent, even blessed, future.

Albany was not Chicago. Indeed, in the Reformed church, Chicago stood for the "west," the residence for the new immigrants from the Netherlands. It was in deference to their new sisters and brothers in the faith that Albanians, along with other eastern classes, were willing to delay union with the German church. The Reformed church as a whole was not ready to join an era of new ecumenism and progressivism.

Martin Marty has refracted American church history at the turn of the century through the lens of "modernity" and constructed a typology around how the various churches responded to the challenge of the new world. Some, caught in the excitement of change, saw in modernity the hand of God and embraced it enthusiastically. Recent immigrants often found it necessary to retreat from the new order into ethnic enclaves in order to survive. Others were more angrily anti-modern.[1]

Albany had been part of the American experiment from the

90

beginning. The classis existed in a culture that did not leave it changed. As the classis approached the turn of the century, it did so with many of its peculiar Reformed tendencies rubbed away, ready to take its place in a more generic "Protestant" world.

That Albany Classis had been swept into the tide of modernity is clear. The Reformed church had evolved into a denomination and the classis had readily participated in the process. The rise of the denomination was itself a product of modernity. Modernity drew reality with clear lines. The "clear and distinct ideas" of Descartes translated into the objectivity of a new science. This led through several twists and turns to an impulse to efficiency and bureaucratization, the very building blocks of a denomination. The classis's own concern with results and numbers reflected modernity's project locally.

And yet the story is not so straightforward. While it will be clear that the classis cannot be viewed as "countermodern," neither can it be seen embracing the enthusiasms of the progressives; there is little evidence that many progressive concerns even came into the purview of the classis. More to the point, the classis continued to do business in the "old" way. Although its delegates fretted about a loss of Reformed "identity," the classis remained distinctively Reformed, especially in its polity.

A Confident Church

As the classis approached the turn into the twentieth century, it had little to fear and much to hope. It, too, could be magnanimous, open, and confident as it observed the surrounding culture. Its "State of Religion" report at the turn of the century reflects a confident church. The classis joined in the celebration of the age. And yet, it sounded caution, too.

The report begins with an indication of what may have been anticipated by many in the larger Christian community as a new century began: "Great expectations were...raised at the beginning of the year by the utterance of some who seemed to think that all energies, divine and human, could be summoned at will and the world set right in a day. This dream has resulted in disappointment." This is poor theology, the classis reminded itself. It is to "outrun the Lord," and to forget that the "operations of the Holy Spirit are not governed by the new Century...." Indeed, the classis recalled, Christ's "personal ministry on earth" was accomplished "not by methods, wise and otherwise, to crowd the ranks of his disciples....Comparatively few...accepted his salvation."

Still, the report could hardly contain itself, its own cautionary words nothwithstanding. The classis gloried in a "gratifying increase in the membership and a still more marked increase in benevolent gifts, showing that the Lord has been present with His people to aid in bringing back the lost ones and enlarging the hearts of His own." In fact, reports from the churches bore out the report's enthusiasm. In the city, the Madison Avenue church increased its benevolent giving by $3,000 over the previous year, and Third doubled its benevolent contributions. More telling, the immigrant churches, Fourth and Holland, were flourishing: Fourth reduced its debt by $1,000 and Holland reported its highest mission giving ever. Some country churches could boast as well: Knox raised its benevolent giving by a quarter over the previous year, and Clarksville enjoyed a large gain in membership. Almost without exception all churches reported harmony, steady attendance, and a sense of spiritual peace and growth.[2]

Maintaining Identity

Was all well in the churches? Perhaps. But the attentive observer begins to notice some quiet changes in the lives of the congregations. They turned, for example, from a strong commitment to the confessions that gave the Reformed churches their identity to a more generic American ecclesiastical identity. The shift is subtle but sure.

A note in the minutes of 1900 remarks that many of the Sunday schools were ordering supplies from local dealers. The churches, perhaps for convenience, found themselves teaching a similar curriculum to other, non-Reformed congregations in and about Albany. This fact prompted the classis to recommend that its Sunday schools order from "our own Board of Publication." By itself, this note might sound inconsequential, but the same report raised a more serious concern:

> ...Is it not time that we seriously consider this subject
> [Catechetics] so that our youth may make a profession of
> their faith with a knowledge of the doctrines of God's Word,
> and thus become loyal and steadfast *to our own
> denomination.*[3]

The loss of importance of a system of catechism is also evident
from continued reports that young people united with the
congregation on profession of faith "from the Sunday School."
Churches often reported that so many scholars had united with
the congregation from its church school. The Sunday school report
to the classis in April, 1903, boasts that the Madison Avenue
church "leads the list of scholars received into the church,
reporting 15." The same report mentions the lack of catechetical
instruction.[4] If youths were educated for membership with
materials purchased locally, and thus not peculiarly "Reformed,"
then a more general, a less focused, less confessionally based
membership would result. That the classis worried about this is
clear from its reports. That it could do much about it seems less
certain.

Indeed, the lack of catechetical instruction was part of a
continuing concern over the lack of preaching on the Heidelberg
Catechism. Almost from its beginning, the classis fretted about
the infrequency with which its pastors heeded the implied
admonition to preach regularly on the Catechism. By 1901, the
classis seemed ready to throw in the towel. At the same meeting
that saw the classis so confident of its future, it also overtured
General Synod to strike "Question 2" of the Constitutional
Inquiries directed to each consistory. Question 2 asked: "Is the
Heidelberg Catechism regularly explained agreeably to the
Constitution of the Reformed (Dutch) Church?"[5] The General
Synod took no action.

The overture reflected the actual practices of the congregations.
In 1906, only two churches, the Holland church and Third,
Albany, answered "yes" to the inquiry about the Catechism.[6] This
was part of a larger trend in the Reformed church. In 1909, a
committee formed by the Particular Synod of Albany reported that
in response to its survey, sixty percent of the churches in the
particular synods of Albany, New Brunswick, and New York

answered "no" to Question 2.[7] The particular synod took no action and referred to an action of the General Synod of 1892:

> Expounding the catechism and catechising the youth of the Church must be left to the conscience of the pastor and judgment of the Church he serves, and to the Classis to which he belongs.[8]

This response did little but reveal that the problem was not isolated to Albany's classis. A "solution" apparently had been found by 1917, when all the churches answered "yes" to Question 2. However, it was a change in the wording that afforded the churches a better conscience. The question now read: "Are the *points of doctrine* contained in the Heidelberg Cathechism explained in your church from time to time as required by the Constitution of the Reformed Church in America?" [emphasis added]. The churches could agree that their pastors covered the "points of doctrine."[9]

Perhaps this tale tells little; after all, the preaching of the Catechism had always been a problem. Coupled with other indications of a loosening of confessional constraints, however, it can indicate a trend. Further indications of a trend show up in the way the classis executed its responsibility to clergy under its care. For example, James S. Kittle received a call from First, Albany, in 1907. He came from the Hudson River Association of Congregational Churches. The classis "heard" him accept "the doctrinal beliefs and the polity of the Reformed Church....A satisfactory statement was made by the brother." There is nothing remarkable in this fact; it continues a long-attested practice of the classis. What is noteworthy, however, is what *isn't* in the classis's minutes. For the first time, the classis did not examine a candidate from outside the Reformed church.[10]

In a related action, four years later the classis overtured the General Synod to drop the requirement that candidates for ministry trained in a non-Reformed church seminary receive a dispensation from the professorial certificate from the General Synod. Instead the classis suggested that any classis be authorized to examine the candidate without a dispensation from the synod.[11] While the synod did not accede, the action suggests that Albany Classis was moving ever so slowly away from a strong denominational identity.

The same movement can be seen in a slightly different matter, an arrangement for a Methodist to become pastor of one of the classis's churches. The churches of Knox and Second, Berne, petitioned the classis in 1917 that they be permitted to join with a Methodist Episcopal church in Knox to hire a minister. The minister was to be Methodist, on the agreement that at the conclusion of the pastorate in question, the three churches would receive a Reformed pastor. The classis granted the request, and one A.V. Patton from the Knox Methodist Episcopal Church was present at a classis meeting and was voted a corresponding delegate in 1918. In fact, Patton made regular reports to the classis of his work and the classis went so far as to write to the superintendant of the Albany District of the Troy Conference of the Methodist Episcopal church to request that Patton be reappointed![12] Readers cognizant of the historical bitterness between the "Arminian Methodists" and the "Reformed Calvinists" would find this arrangement remarkable indeed.

A Polity that Stuck

This is not to suggest that the classis was ready to fade from the scene as its churches became ever more a part of a generic American Protestantism. The classis continued to evolve in its polity. It retained a strong connection with the churches. However, that connection came to have less and less to do with the internal life of the churches and with the discipline of their members. As the century turned, there is almost no mention of disciplinary action of church members referred to the classis. Two reasons suggest themselves. First, the matter of discipline could have been shared less frequently with the classis. However, church polity had not changed, and, given the relatively constant nature of human personalities, had the churches disciplined, one would expect to find appeals in classis records. A second explanation seems more plausible: the churches simply disciplined less. Of course, the classis retained a firm hand with the churches, but now that firmness takes a slightly different turn. The classis always superintended calls and kept a close eye on the relation of a church to its pastor. In 1900, the first mention of the appointment of a supervisor to a vacant church appears when

"The Rev. J. Van Westenberg was appointed Classical Supervisor of the Second Ref. Church of Bethlehem."[13] The arrangement became more official in 1908 when the General Synod proposed to change the Constitution so that a classis could appoint one of its ministers to be the president of the consistory of a vacant church. The classis agreed so readily and so promptly that it appointed several of its ministers to be presidents of the consistories of vacant churches, even though the change would not be official for another year![14]

This action was to have consquences only a year later, when trouble was reported from the church in Union. The classis had formed a committee to investigate what had been happening in Union between the church and its supply pastor, Fletcher Lehman. In fact, Mr. Lehman and his elder had earlier reported the termination of the arrangement between Lehman and the church. The classis, appealing to General Synod's action to empower classes to appoint presidents of consistories, appointed Adrian Westveer as president at Union. At the same time, the classis requested that Union change its method of electing consistory. At the time, Union had used the "third method," by which the consistory chose its own successors. The classis wanted the church to use the "second method" described in the Constitution, by which members of the congregation chose the consistory without nomination by the current consistory.

Union concurred, and Westveer reported to the next meeting of the classis that a new consistory had been elected at Union. However, Westveer received several protests from members at Union on the election and installation of the new consistory. The classis declared the protests invalid and ordered Westveer to install the new consistory.[15] Albany Classis retained a strong supervisory role over its churches.

A more instructive, and more ennobling, story emerges from the relation of the classis to its church in Westerlo. The classis was happy to report in 1895 that it had received only a statistical report from the church in Westerlo. The classis viewed this as progress, "for it is some years since we have heard from this church." Indeed the church claimed a gain of eleven members which "...proves that the condition of the Westerlo chu. is not hopeless."[16]

But there was trouble on the horizon. By spring, 1899, the classis reported that no preaching services had been held in Westerlo for a year, and it formed a committee to investigate. The committee reported at the next classis meeting that it had not only investigated the situation at Westerlo, but at Onesquethaw as well. The classis instructed the committee to widen its scope and look into the churches at Clarksville and New Salem. Evidently, the classis was concerned for the state of several of its smaller churches.[17] This concern proved well founded, for by the following April (1900), New Salem related that it hadn't had a pastor since September 1, and the church had been open only five times since. Westerlo, in the meantime, reported no services at all, because of "death and removals," and saw "no prospect of having a regular minister."[18] In 1901, Onesquethaw reported that it was supplied every other Sunday by a Presbyterian minister from New Scotland. It couldn't afford to hold weekly services.[19]

In December, 1900, as a result of the struggles of these churches, the classis instructed its Committee on Vacant Churches to investigate the union of the Westerlo church with the Onesquethaw churches. Or, if that did not appear feasible, to look into a union between the Westerlo church and the Presbyterian church in Rensselaerville.[20]

In 1901, the classis took a small action. The Westerlo church, represented by two elders, reported that it had now been closed for three years. The classis resolved to seek a stated supply for the summer of 1902.[21] Little happened and an elder from Westerlo reported to the classis that there "seems to be no hope." This time the classis sent its entire Committee on Vacant Churches to Westerlo to meet on "some afternoon" and to hold evening services to "learn prospects." The classis empowered the committee to confer with authorities from other denominations to seek a possible union between Westerlo and some other church.[22] E.P. Johnson, pastor of First, Albany, reported for the committee that it had met with the Westerlo church and had recommended that a student from the seminary be sent for the summer. A student was found and worked in the summer of 1904. An elder from Westerlo could speak confidently in the fall of 1904 of the work of the student. The church now was in a position to raise $200 and to furnish a parsonage for the support of a minister.[23]

Finally, in April, 1906, the classis approved the call of Westerlo on the Rev. James P. Bryant. Sadly, the arrangement lasted a little less than three years before the classis dissolved the relation between Bryant and the church. The reason given the classis was poor health of the pastor.[24] It was not until 1915 that the church could report that Donald Boyce, a student at Franklin and Marshall, had been supplying them to good report. The classis set up a committee to outline and supervise a course of study for Boyce. The classis promised to examine him and to apply to the General Synod for dispensation. That classis did examine Boyce and applied for a dispensation (although, interestingly, the classis examined Boyce in all subjects *before* it received a dispensation from the General Synod!). Boyce then served Westerlo for ten years. (He was to return as a stated supply from 1939-1945, and as pastor from 1945-1961.)[25]

Westerlo's story is interesting not simply because the classis did something to rescue a struggling church. In fact, it might be wondered just what the classis did. However, the story illustrates how a church could continue to exist even when it held no services, by retaining elders who represented it to the classis. And the classis could keep the church alive, if only on life support, until with some help it could call a pastor once again.

Likewise, the classis continued its strong supervision of candidates for ministry. Two signal instances occurred in the time under our consideration, one with a happy resolution, one with a less than pleasant result. First, the latter. In 1904, a member of First, Albany, Andrew Vander Wart, applied for a dispensation from academic studies to be ordained "to better enable him to perform the duties of Chaplain to the Albany Pentitentiary." The classis made application to the General Synod, and synod granted the dispensation.[26] However, the special committee that the classis had formed to receive Vander Wart's request could make no recommendation, and the classis instructed the committee to report a procedure. The committee reported meeting with those who had the power to appoint the prison chaplain only to discover that ordination was not essential to the appointment. In fact, it was thought that the chaplain's influence could be greater if he remained a layman. The committee put the matter "plainly" to Vander Wart, and he agreed to withdraw his request for ordination.[27] Why the classis hadn't asked these questions before it applied for a dispensation remains unanswered.

But the story doesn't end there. The following year (1905) someone in the classis reported seeing a newspaper notice that "A.M. Vander Wart" was to become a minister in the Reformed church, to be ordained in December or early January. This was news to the classis. The classis voted to ask Vander Wart if he had indeed authorized such an article in the public press and to put it to him "plainly" that if so he had prejudiced his request for ordination. The classis received no reply to its request and formed yet another committee to investigate. By May, 1906, the classis was ready to inform the General Synod that it would not avail themselves of the dispensation granted Vander Wart.[28]

The second instance led to a more positive result. In 1911, the New Baltimore church called W. R. Torrens, a Presbyterian, to its pulpit. The classis agreed to receive him provided he undertake eighteen months of study in theology and church government under the tutelage of Dr. E. W. Miller and J. P. Brown. He agreed, was received into the classis, and the call approved. Two years later, the classis "discharged the condition" on Torrens. The committee that had been supervising his work told the classis that he had done well in his studies. The classis then declared him a member in full and regular standing.[29]

Under Discipline: C.P. Evans

It has been noted that the Albany Classis was less involved in the discipline of church members. It remained intimately involved in the life of its clergy, however. So it was in the sad case of the Rev. C. P. Evans. In 1903, at a special meeting of the classis, the body noted, under "miscellaneous business," rumors "derogatory to the ministerial standing of C. P. Evans." The classis appointed a committee to investigate.[30]

Within two months the committee returned to report that the rumors were of alleged financial chicanery worked by Mr. Evans on an older couple, Mr. and Mrs. Simeon Fairlee from Lisha's Kill. The committee recounted that "while the evidence obtainable might not suffice for conviction in a criminal court it is more than sufficient to convince us of the most serious deriliction from the law of Christian integrity and kindness."

Just here, however, things began to bog down on the classis's own procedures. The investigative committee recommended that Evans be summoned for trial. The classis referred its advices to the standing committee on Judicial Business. That committee reported, however, that it had no evidence against Evans. It could recommend no summons, but promised to investigate further.[31]

The Judicial Business Committee returned five months later still frustrated. It reported that no one had offered to come before the classis to make a formal charge against Evans; that the aggrieved parties had been advised that they would most likely get nowhere in either criminal or civil court; and that the investigative committee had interviewed Evans and had knowledge that the standing committee still didn't have (evidently the left hand still didn't know what the right hand was doing). Still, the standing committee recommended that Evans be summoned with the additional note that he "be requested to appear before the classis and explain the alleged wrongs with which he is informally charged." Evans did not appear in person, but sent along a letter "presenting excuses for seeming wrongs done." That was not sufficient, and the classis set up yet another committee to formulate charges against Evans.[32]

Shortly after this action, Evans requested of the classis that he be dismissed to the Presbytery of Binghamton. The classis could only refuse, since it was "not at liberty" to dismiss him so long as he was under investigation. The new committee meanwhile discovered that Mrs. Fairlee was willing and able to testify. Mr. Fairlee, on the other hand, was not physically able to take the stand publicly. The Fairlee's lawyer, with their consent, was prepared to turn over relevant notes and letters to the classis. Other interested parties were also ready to testify to the classis.

The classis then charged Evans with breaking the eighth commandment, citing the Heidelberg Catechism's interpretation of the commandment. Specifically, the classis cited Evans with defrauding the Fairlees on two financial notes. "With these wicked tricks and deceptions you are charged and with gaining the confidence of Mr. and Mrs. Simeon Fairlee as a minister of Christ and praying with them and at the same time deceiving and defrauding them."[33]

The classis set a date for trial two weeks hence, but when the day arrived, Evans was not present. Instead, he sent another letter stating that his son was ill and that he had to be out of town. He included a letter stating his defense against the charges. The classis judged that it could not try Evans in absentia until he had been cited twice. The classis sent its sympathies to Evans on his son's illness and set a new trial date.

The new date arrived, a month later. Evans himself began the judicial session by entering an objection: the offense with which he was charged was a private and not a public offense, and thus not to be handled publicly. The chair ruled that the classis was required to take congnizance of what had come to it by general rumor, and thus that the offense was indeed public.

The classis tried the case and found Evans guilty of the general charge. It declared Evans suspended from the ministry "until such time as he shall give satisfactory evidence to this classis of repentance and restitution." The classis further voted that the action "be not published upon a written pledge of Mr. Evans not to exercise the functions of the Christian ministry during his suspension."[34]

Evans appealed the decision to the particular synod on the following grounds:

a. The classis confused a public with a private offense. At issue was a business transaction that could have been settled amicably according to the dictates of Matthew 18.

b. The offense in question happened prior to the two-year statute of limitations deliniated in the Reformed church's Constitution.

c. The classis assumed "jurisdiction of doubtful propriety." If there were matters to be complained, the proper forum was a court of law.

d. The classis had rejected "as of no account" the power of attorney given to Evans by Mr. Fairlee.

e. The classis rendered its judgment contrary to the weight of the evidence developed in the trial.

The appeal to the particular synod failed because Evans once again did not appear. However, Evans convinced the synod to reconsider and to hear his appeal. The classis protested that the synod thereby overstepped its authority. Classis argued that the appeal had been reliquished, not by the action of the synod, but by the Constitution itself. The classis had lost all patience with Evans, so that when he claimed that he "mistakenly" missed the meeting of synod, the classis seriously doubted Evans's sincerity. In any event, the synod granted the classis's request and dismissed the appeal. Nor, for that matter, would the General Synod be any more congenial to Evans's appeal.

Still, Evans didn't let matters rest. He appealed to the civil courts. In 1906, a New York State judge had issued a Writ of Certiorari, which demanded the records of the case. The classis produced them for the court and proceeded to hire an attorney. Nothing happened, and three years later Evans showed up at a classis meeting, requesting that the classis rescind its discipline. Classis saw no reason to do so but gave Evans five minutes to state his case.

Evans fired one more arrow from his quiver. He applied to a civil court for a writ of mandamus. The writ would have overturned the action of the classis. But no writ was issued, and there the matter ended.[35]

This case was the last public disciplinary procedure of any kind in the classis until late in the twentieth century.

A Church for its Country

This chapter began with the observation that the classis was becoming a part of a bold, progressivist country, a country with a manifest destiny. It is fitting to conclude this chapter by offering an unusual glimpse of how the classis viewed the life of the country and the place of the faith as the country entered America's century. The occasion is the assasination of President McKinley and the accession of Theodore Roosevelt to the office of president.

On September 24, 1901, the classis paused to articulate a special resolution on the event of the hour. The classis expressed "deep sorrow" on the tragic death of the president. The classis then expressed an

appreciation of the exalted character which he bore and the

eminent services which he rendered. In public life faithful in the discharge of every duty, meeting the momentous issues which he was called to face, bravely and with great wisdom, his life was a consecrated service for his country's good. In his home life there was revealed a domestic relation of great tenderness and beauty. Of deep religious convictions, he lived an exemplary Christian life; with Christian fortitude he bore the sufferings inflicted upon him, and he met death sustained by an unfaltering trust in God.

The classis paid tribute to a president who expressed Christian virtues, who was exemplary in his home life, who was deeply one of their own faith. Likewise, the church enjoyed a confident connection with a government it could trust.

But the classis did not simply eulogize McKinley. It was with pride that it could look to McKinley's successor. Roosevelt was a son of New York State, a former governor who worshiped in Albany's First Church, and who once had invited the entire classis to meet with him in the Executive Chamber in Albany. Roosevelt was one "well fitted" to become president, and so to "continue the policy inaugurated by our late President for 'the peace, prosperity and honor of our beloved country.'" The classis expressed its appreciation of Roosevelt's interest in the Reformed church. It offered him "our loyalty and earnest support, and promise him our prayers for God's blessing to attend him in the discharge of the trying duties" as president. One senses that this is the classis in one of its prouder hours.[36]

Still, the classis as an institution would be selective about the civic issues that warranted its attention. It would, for example, have very little to say about the United States's entrance into a world war in 1917. It confined its few official remarks to notices that a particular minister or another had served as chaplain. The classis, it appears, was content to retreat into the mildly evangelical world it had chosen to inhabit. In fact, the classis entered a time of silence in the midst of a growing storm among America's churches. And that is the story for the following chapter.

VII
The Sound of Silence
(1919-1941)

With the advantage of distance, the observer has watched the Classis of Albany enter what might be called the Protestant consensus, or the way of the broad middle, albeit with some of the sharper edges of its Calvinist heritage still adhering. This will take a sharper focus as the classis enters the inter-war period of the 1920s and '30s. But the story is not simply "more of the same." Several subtle shifts will occur in the life of the classis as it lives out its way of being church in its local, trans-parish expression. This chapter describes those developments.

However, the classis will sound an odd dissonance in the broader culture of Protestantism. Martin Marty has described the final break-up of the Protestant consensus as that broad ecclesiastical community engaged in two major disputes that tore at denominations across ecclesiastical boundaries. The first, most popularly remembered by the "Scopes trial" over the teaching of evolution in public schools, exploded into a modernist-fundamentalist divide. The second approached with the coming of the Second World War and had Protestants splitting over the issue of war and peace.[1] In contrast to the "noise of conflict" at large in American Protestantism, there is little evidence of the conflict within the classis itself. What does the (relative) silence mean?

Marty cites a speech given by soon to be president Warren G. Harding, on May 14, 1920, just three weeks before the Republican National Convention. The speech measured the mood of a country just recovering from its first engagement in a world war. The speech was remembered for its phrase, "not nostrums, but normality," but it also included the phrase, "not experiment, but equipoise."[2] Robert and Helen Lynd in their study of the largely

Protestant Middletown, quoted a Muncie, Indiana, editorial, "Why Go to Church?" The middle-American editorialist answered: "In the church of the right kind there is an atmosphere of soul peace and contentment that comes with more nearly meeting human needs and longings for better things than anything the week days hold."[3] Between the wars, the Classis of Albany sounds like nothing less than an attempt to maintain "normalcy."

Membership loss and gain and the Progress Campaign

The classis expressed its concern for normalcy in two State of Religion reports at the onset of this period. In 1919, the classis reported a decrease of five in total membership. Worse yet, it had received only 133 members in 1919, compared with 269 in 1918. "The difference between the figures of the two years should give us grave concern. Surely the question is a pointed one—are we faithfully meeting our responsibilities as ministers and elders of the Church of Jesus Christ? The reports of the churches well emphasize the need of a deeper consecration to the interests of the kingdom on the part of us all."[4] The following year, the classis again reported that the statistics for the year were "not encouraging" but detailed losses in "almost every particular." The classis urged the churches to "look into their methods of work." "Our educational system must be modernized, our pastoral reading and study must be of a solid character so that our preaching will be instructive as well as inspiring. And would it not be well if the pastoral instruction of youth were better attended to?"[5] The comment is instructive in that it urges a "modernization," but it also sets up a contrast between inspiration and instruction. One continues to hear Reformed echoes of the need not only for well-informed preaching, but well-informed laity, from youth onward.

The same report urged the implementation of the Progress Campaign as one way to stem the losses in the church. The Progress Campaign began in 1918 as a denominational program jointly proposed by the boards of the Reformed church to increase the influence of the church through an evangelistic effort that would increase church membership by 25,000 the first year,

30,000 the second year, and so on; increase the "efficiency" of religious education; urge systematic reading of church periodicals; recruit at least one candidate for ministry from every church; emphasize stewardship; and stress both domestic and foreign missions.[6]

By 1919's General Synod, the program had become the Progress Campaign, which adopted a financial goal of 5.5 million dollars over the next five years; a "go to church campaign"; and a stewardship educational campaign. The campaign evolved into a separate church structure, complete with its own Progress Council, annual reports to the General Synod, and representatives in every classis.[7]

Albany Classis endorsed the campaign. The first mention of this ambitious denominational program comes at the Fall, 1919, session of the classis. The classis then met in special session in January, 1920, to endorse the campaign and to accept the apportionment for the classis, which was $27,960. Responsibility for this amount was distributed among the churches, with the greater share to come from Albany's First and Madison Avenue churches (together almost $18,000 of the total).[8] The classis continued its support (at least verbally) when it "heartily endorsed" the Progress Council message of March, 1928, and its "plan of advance." In fact, the classis appointed a committee of four ministers and four "laymen" to act with the full power of classis in carrying out the recommendations of the Progress Council.[9]

In fact, by 1925, the classis was exultant at the "results of the past year's activity." It reported "progress" in all areas, and "efficiency in all lines of activity." But a sober look at the statistics for the years provokes the observer to wonder. In 1919, the classis reported its communicant membership at 3,356. In 1924, the membership was reported at 3,068, or a loss of 288. True, the classis had received 773 new members in the first half of the decade. It is also true that churches would periodically "revise the rolls" as they took an honest look at their membership. Still, the results could hardly have been what had been hoped. Each year the churches had collectively received between 130 and 190 members. The classis did have a bit of a revival toward the end of the decade: in 1928, it received 519 new members; in 1929, 294; and in 1930, 244. Thus, by the end of the decade, the classis could rejoice modestly in a gain of almost 300 members. This is still less than ten percent, and scarcely the numbers hoped for by the General Synod as it set out on its campaign.

The statistical report of benevolent giving in the classis tells a different story. It is not clear what the nearly $28,000 goal was meant to encompass. But the classis increased its giving to denominational programs from $13,115 in 1919 to $19,104 in 1924, or a growth of 45.6 percent. The total increase for the five years added together was $27,389. Whether this matched the goal the classis adopted in 1920, it was a significant result.

The classis engaged in one other flurry of activity in the middle of the decade that hoped for much. It began afresh on a new project in church extension. In the fall of 1927 it established a new committee (that included the synod missionary, Donald Boyce, a member of Albany's classis) to study areas in the city of Albany that might be receptive to a new church. The committee was to conduct surveys and to look for potential property. To signal its seriousness, the classis prepared to levy a one cent per member assessment, to shoulder the initial costs of obtaining property, and to pay the interest on moneys borrowed for purchase.

By the spring of 1928, the committee had found three possible sites. One, not chosen, was in the New Scotland area, near the corner of Whitehall and Slingerlands roads (near where the Bethany church was to settle in the 1950s). The classis chose instead a location in Elsmere, along Delaware Avenue, halfway between the Normanskill viaduct and the D&H railroad crossing, in what was a suburb of Albany, and not far from the Delmar church. However, as a result of "new developments," the classis rescinded its action in 1929, and nothing came of the project.[10]

The observer senses that the Progress Campaign did in fact model a means for the classis to continue its effort to maintain "normalcy" in its little piece of the Protestant empire. In 1933, the classis acted to hold a rally in the fall of that year in an Albany church to promote interest in the denominational program. It also voted to sponsor a devotional retreat for ministers, officers, and organizational heads of the various congregations, to be held in a suburban church.[11] One wonders what suburban church it had in mind, since only Delmar stood in what could be called a suburb, unless one places Third and Sixth in the "suburban" areas of the city. Then, in 1940, the classis voted to hold a meeting of the churches in the interests of foreign missions in November of that year.[12]

Depression in the Church

Whatever the "new developments" mentioned above were, in 1928-29 the classis was entering a sobering time. It was, of course, the beginning of the decade of the Great Depression. Still, even before the crash that was to echo around the world, the classis was sending signals of concern. At its October 15, 1929, meeting, the classis set up a committee "to study the whole church situation within the bounds of the classis in order that classis may know what conditions prevail today."[13] One lookd in vain for the text of that report. The minutes do not mention its ever having been given.

Throughout the thirties, however, the classis fretted over the state of its churches. Of particular concern was the apparent decrease in Sunday school enrollment. One report found the reason in the small number of children born in "our Protestant communities." The report continued, perhaps prophetically, that this fact "strikes at our very existence." It added, caustically, that there "is no need for passing laws for birth control for self destruction is evident." The relevant paragraph ends: "No children. Not wanted."[14]

Even a modestly hopeful report at the end of the interwar period sent up alarm signals and placed a cautious conclusion on the two decades dominated denominationally by the Progress Campaign. The 1940 State of Religion report detailed a need for

...a careful scrutiny in the spiritual life of the church to see if in our anxiety for larger figures of those uniting and the raising of money we are overlooking the building of the kingdom within our own churches, so that those who once caught the vision and later found it growing dim and dropped by the wayside. It is a vain and futile thing to make drives and canvasses and spend much effort in bringing the lost within the church, to have in turn those who once saw the light have it grow dim after a few years.

The classis had enjoyed a hefty growth in the number of new members that year, but it went on to worry that the churches were losing as many as they were gaining.[15] This caution faintly echoes the tone of the 1830 report issued at the height of the Second Great Awakening. The classis was interested enough in growth in numbers, but it continued to worry that concentration on "drives and canvasses" distracted the churches from the necessary work of educating their members.

While the Depression might be an apt metaphor to describe the mood of the classis, the primary effects of the Depression itself were felt by the churches. The collapsing American economy dominated their environment. The classis had enjoyed a steady increase in giving through the twenties. In fact, on the eve of the Depression, the classis was upbeat. Over the past decade, more churches had joined the "$1,000-circle," thereby reducing the disproportion of giving to the denomination by the First, Albany, and Madison Avenue churches.[16]

Two and a half years later, however, the story was different. In the first explicit mention of the economic Depression, the classis resolved that "in view of existing conditions of unrest and economic depression...it would be good and altogether proper to have a national day of humiliation and prayer...."[17] The way in which the churches were allocating their money had become a matter of serious concern. Churches strapped for cash were dipping into offerings given for benevolences to keep their own congregations solvent. This practice provoked a reprimand from the classis that it disapproved of "any diversion of Benevolent Funds by local churches," and the classis exhorted the churches to "adhere to the strictest ethical practices in the administration of these funds." The classis also told the churches that quarterly payments were to be continued to the denomination's Progress Council "or to the Boards for which they are intended."[18] In these matters the classis attempted to act in concert, as one body, but it was also cautious not to overstep. It "urged" and "recommended" to the churches. It even voted that a copy of the action be sent to each of the churches. But the classis did not require the churches to take the requested action.

There was little the classis could do to help its churches through the economic crisis. They simply had to ride out the storm together. In 1933, giving for denominational purposes dropped by 35 percent; and for local congregations by 14 percent, and the downward trend continued. In 1935, the State of Religion report rather wistfully hoped that the "low point had been reached."[19]

"Efficiency and Economy"

The appearance of a new language in various reports, classical and denominational, has been noted. Words like "modernization" and "efficiency" had crept in. The organization itself had become the subject of attention. Could churches be up to date in their operation? This was a startling change of language, and it had its effect on how the classis would operate.

In fact, the classis's approach to modernity is reflected in its language. In the early 1930s, the classis overtured the Particular Synod of Albany for a realignment of classical boundaries. The particular synod was sympathetic, but little came of the initiative (one of a set which continued throughout the history of the classis; with two notable exceptions, little came of any of them). The point, however, is the language the classis used in its request. Classical boundaries were to be redrawn, Albany claimed, "for greater efficiency and economy."[20]

The careful reader of the minutes can watch the classis ever so slowly trying to move away from its rather awkward way of being church together. While one must be careful of arguments from silence, one still notes with interest that after the 1903 affair with Evans, the classis did not for many years involve itself in a disciplinary procedure. And no record exists of classical involvement in the discipline of a church member after the turn of the century.

Two other notes, however small, are telling, as the classis withdraws more from the local congregations, and looks to reduce its own work. The first involves two actions that affected the review of consistorial activities. In 1919, the classis considered a proposal that a committee of classis would no longer examine the minutes of the consistories. Instead, each consistory was to examine the minutes of the church that preceded it in the roll of the churches. The proposal was accepted with this change: it would be the minutes of the boards of elders that would be examined.[21] Apparently, the classis continued to review consistorial minutes. A decade later, however, the classis took two actions that indicated its discomfort with a strong oversight. It noted, first, that the "approval or non-approval of Consistorial Minutes has been based upon faithfulness in asking the constitutional questions and in opening and closing each session with prayer...." Then, to add icing, the classis overtured the General Synod to change the method of constitutional inquiries so that the inquiries would be made by printed blanks given to consistories and returned to the stated clerk. The General Synod did not agree.[22] Albany Classis had taken the initiative in the interest of efficiency and economy. It was a signal retreat.

A second telling change in its method of operation had the classis consolidating its meetings around the approval of calls and services of installation. Previously, the classis would meet first to approve the call and, perhaps at the same meeting, establish the service of installation—who would preside, preach, read the formulae, etc. Then, at the appropriate date, the classis would meet to ordain and/or to install the minister. In about the mid-1920s, the classis began to accomplish all this at one time, the day or evening of the ordination/installation![23]

In fact, things got so "efficient" that when First and Madison Avenue merged following the tragic loss of Madison Avenue's building to fire, the pastor of the newly merged church, Stephen James, declined to be installed (the merger required a new call). That seemed fair enough. But in the meantime, the "new" First Church had called an associate pastor, Bertram Atwood. The classis voted to waive his installation as well![24]

While this change is significant, it was not abrupt. The classis continued its strong review of the pastors within its bounds. The aforementioned M. Stephen James, who later became president of the General Synod and president of New Brunswick Theological Seminary, had been an established pastor of a Methodist church in nearby Massachusetts. Yet, the classis required him to undergo an examination prior to approving his call to First Church.[25] That the classis did not perform this duty lightly is evidenced by two other instances that brought varying results. In 1924, the classis received J.J. Gould to pastor the Jerusalem and Onesquethaw churches. Gould was a Baptist who presented a letter of dismission from a Baptist congregation, a certificate of ordination from a "Council of Messengers," and a diploma from the Practical Bible Training School of Binghamton, New York. Gould also presented a doctrinal statement in accord with the requirements of the RCA Constitution. The Constitution required that a classis cannot receive a minister or candidate from any Christian body maintaining doctrines that differ from the Standards of the RCA "without a complete and explicit declaration in writing on his part, that he renounces such doctrines as are contrary to the Word of God and to such Standards." Gould went on to pastor one other Reformed congregation before returning to the Baptists.[26]

A less happy resolution occurred in the case of Rufus Lefevre. In 1928, the Clarksville and Westerlo consistories requested that Lefevre be approved as a pulpit supply for their churches. The classis had some questions. It interviewed him and agreed that the churches could engage him for one year. However, they were to report to the following meeting of the classis, there to request a renewal of the contract. Furthermore, the classis allowed Lefevre to administer the sacraments, but it emphasized that he do so in accordance with the RCA Liturgy. Still further, he was to be subject to the advice and supervision of the classical supervisor (Donald Boyce, the former pastor of the two churches).

The arrangement didn't last until the next meeting. Within three months, the classis had to meet to mediate a fresh dispute in the churches. It was reported that Lefevre had alienated a substantial number from the Clarksville church and had become the source of dissension in both churches. He had brought twenty-nine (!) charges against Boyce. On request, he could substantiate none to the classis.

The classis "advised and demanded" the immediate termination of the contract between Lefevre and the churches, but apparently the churches did not comply. Two months later, the classis summoned the entire consistory at Westerlo to appear at its fall session to answer to that body why they had acted "contrary to the precise order of the classis." Classis warned the consistories

of the two churches that they would held personally liable for
money expended in violation of an order from the classis.
The classis action did not go down well, at least in Westerlo.
Their entire consistory, as well as the church treasurer, resigned
in protest. The classis had to appoint a committee with the full
power of classis to call a congregational meeting to elect a new
consistory.[27] Retreat as it might for the sake of "efficiency and
economy," the classis retained considerable bite.

City, Country—and Suburb

It has already been shown that the classis understood itself to
be a confederation of city and rural churches. This understanding
began to shift slightly in this period of "normalcy." We have cited
statistics that divided the population of the classis roughly in half
between city and country over most of the classis's life. This
division had changed rather strikingly by 1910, when the classis
counted 61 percent of its members in city churches. By 1920, the
proportion had risen to 64.5 percent, and it was to remain well
above 50 percent until the mid-1940s. From there the proportion
held by the city churches would decline to around 30 percent in
1970.

In part, the strength of the city churches held because six
relatively strong congregations remained intact until a period of
consolidation began when Madison Avenue united with First
following the fire. Then, too, suburbanization had just begun.

But the strength was not just in numbers. First and Madison
Avenue continued to give a disproportion of the classis's
contributions to denominational causes. In 1919, for example, the
two churches gave about $10,200 of the classical total of $13,115.
Meanwhile, "Delmar heads the list of the village or country
churches with $425.[28] The classis was a body of a few relatively
strong, and many much smaller churches. Given that disparity, it
is remarkable that the classis maintained its "parity of ministry."
One gets little sense that the larger churches held sway over the
smaller ones.

And yet, the classis noted already in 1929 that change was in
the wind, when First, Albany, reported that it was experiencing
the problems of a "downtown church." The specific problem

mentioned was decreasing membership. It also noted that Madison Avenue was "becoming a downtown church" as well.[29]

Furthermore, the first use of the term "suburb" appeared during this period. In 1926, the classis noted that "Delmar is rapidly becoming a very desirable and growing Suburban Town and the Reformed Church is evidently awake to its opportunity."[30] Whether that was the case is open to question. It was not until the 1950s and 60s that the classis started two new churches in suburban areas, and the rural churches were not located in areas where suburbs later sprang up. The greater number of suburban churches did not become part of the classis until the 1970s, when the break up of what had been Saratoga Classis added several larger suburban churches to Albany's rolls.

Some Noise

As noted at the outset of this chapter, the silence of the classis was only relative. The classis had a good deal to say about several public issues. It did not reflect the internal disputes that ended the Protestant consensus. Instead, it joined its voice to those issues that had traditionally united the Protestant front: sabbatarianism, prohibition, and opposition to such public immoralities as gambling.

Already in 1919, the classis wrote to the governor of New York asking him to veto bills that allowed motion pictures to open on Sundays and that gave permission for Sunday baseball.[31] If this move seems rather an empty gesture to late twentieth century church folk, one need but recall that while Theodore Roosevelt resided in the governor's mansion, the classis had a very congenial relationship with New York State's governor.

In fact, it is in a resolution on Sabbath observance that something of the classis's theology of society can be understood. In 1931, the classis resolved "that the classis urge the churches to proclaim strict Sabbath observance and obedience to law as fundamental in building and holding that public conscience that will preserve our nation. The Gospel standard for the individual is rigid self-control in fellowship with Christ."[32] The goal was the preservation of the nation. Old Calvinist strains of "obedience" echoed. So did the notion of law, even Sabbath law, as essential to the life not only of individuals, but of an entire nation. The notion of theocracy is not far distant from such reflections. At the same time, the individual is not lost to sight but called to "rigid self-control" albeit in "fellowship with Christ."

The classis also had a bit to say about another common target of evangelical/Protestant America, gambling. In the era under consideration, the classis, in conjunction with the denomination, began to take formal cognizance of "public morals" in the form of committees and/or agents. In 1928, the classis's agent on Public Morals had it adopt a position favoring "the most searching investigation of the baseball gambling pool."[33]

It was Prohibition, however, that claimed much of the classis's attention. Soon following the passage of the eighteenth amendment to the U.S. Constitution, the classis urged the state governor to use his influence to effect the passage of the Thompson McNab Prohibition Enforcement Measure.[34] By 1922, New York State had enacted the Mullen Gage State Prohibition Law that banned the manufacture, sale, importation, and transportation of liquor for use as a beverage. That law did not go down well among many powers in the state, and a move was soon afoot to repeal it. In April, 1923, the classis spoke as forcefully as it could to urge New York State's Assembly (the lower house of the legislature) not to repeal the law. It was repealed that June, anyway.[35] That did not stop the classis. By October, it was ready to "go on record" in support of the eighteenth amendment, the Volstead Act enforcing the amendment at the federal level, and the enactment by the state legislature of the enforcement of the Volstead Act.[36]

Still the issue vexed the classis, and its statements grew stronger in following years. By 1924, the classis "denounced the frequent statement that our prohibition laws cannot be enforced."[37] It was the following year that the classis could contain itself no longer and issued its most detailed official comment:

> In view of the serious condition of lawlessness and open
> defiance of law that exists in our country and especially as

regards the 18th amendment to the Federal Constitution and the consequent Volstead Act and since it seems to your committee the most glaring spirit of defiance is to be charged against our own Empire State because of its continued failure not only to work in harmony with the law and spirit of our Federal Constitution but also its continued attitude of antagonism against the same as again evidenced by the refusal of our last legislature to pass even a fair enforcement measure, and since we as Classis of Albany represent in a special way the Capital District which is at least the law making center of the Empire State, it is the feeling of your committee that we as ministers and elders of the Churches of the Albany Classis should go on record as unalterably opposed to the attitude taken by our legislature and which is generally known as being the stand also of our Governor.

Furthermore, the classis communicated its displeasure to the General Synod, requesting it to express its opposition "hoping and praying that the Empire State may soon come from under the domination of the defiant law breaking element now in political control." General Synod responded by "deploring that aggressive disregard of law and decency," and by pledging itself to renew efforts to the effect that only candidates be elected who support the eighteenth amendment, "especially in New York, where the State is in this regard willfully neglecting its duty."[38]

This is hardly a church retreating from the public realm. Where the issue hit home, and where the classis was certain that it was representing the interests of the gospel, it was not hesitant to enter the public fray, to an extent that can only result in partisan politics. What has come to be called "one-issue" politics was not strange to the Reformed church at the height of Prohibition.

In one other area, the classis had a bit to say. In the period between the wars, what Marty calls "original stock Protestantism" were "enthusiastic supporters" of the cause of peace. This was to culminate in the Kellogg-Briand Peace Pact, or the Pact of Paris, outlawing international war and signed by fifteen nations in August, 1928.[39] The peace movement took hold with many in the Reformed church in the late 20s and the 30s.[40] Early on, in 1923, the classis was moved to support the cause. Again it could put on record an action to "assure our Government officials that America supports them in the efforts that have been made to adjust international relationships, and will support them in whatever future steps may be necessary to protect Christian minorities and bring abiding justice and peace among nations."[41]

Whether a small confederation of churches in the corner of one state had any muscle to flex, it nevertheless saw itself as a guardian of public morals. It had become part and parcel of mainstream American Protestantism.

An American Church

Indeed, Albany Classis could view itself as a church that was a part of a larger church in a very American context. Two other actions evidence this fact, one ecclesiastical, the other confessional.

As it had before, and as it would twice again in this century, the General Synod contemplated union with its sister denomination, the Presbyterians. In 1930, Albany Classis endorsed the proposed union.[42] Nothing came of the effort, but the classis's endorsement showed its identification with a greater Protestant consensus. The irony, of course, is that at that very time that consensus was breathing its last.

Confessionally, the classis voted approval of the proposed change in Article 36 of the Confession of Faith (the so-called "Belgic Confession"). The article had to do with "Civil Magistrates," or the powers of government in a nation. Its claim that the state exercised an "office" not only to act as watchguard over public morality, but that it was also to "prevent and remove all idolatry and false religion" had been difficult to affirm in the American context of the "separation of church and state." The General Synod proposed the deletion of the phrase that had the "Magistrates" removing and preventing all idolatry and false worship "that the kingdom of the antichrist may be thus destroyed, and the kingdom of Christ promoted." The change was not to be ratified by the classes of the denomination, but Albany's approval showed this classis consciously aware that it was indeed a member of an "American" church.[43]

VIII
An Activist Classis
(1941-1978)

The previous chapter showed the Classis of Albany standing apart from the controversies that shook the Protestant consensus. Soon after the outbreak of the Second World War, this attitude changed. The classis entered a period in which it engaged in several controversies that took hold in the Reformed Church in America. Indeed, this history will conclude with an account of the role played by the classis in the affirmation of the ordination of women to all offices of the church, a debate that dragged over decades. But the period between the Second World War and the late 1970s was more than a time of convulsion in one small middle-of-the-road denomination. It was also a time of national upheaval and self-doubt characterized by the onset of the Civil Rights movement in the 1950s and the national agony of the Vietnam experience in the 1960s and 70s. The classis found itself caught in the maelstrom of events. It did not remain passive. In fact, to an extent largely, it became an "activist" classis.

Denominational Brush-fires

Almost coincidentally with America's entry into World War II, the classis found itself caught up in small battles that were beginning to break out in the Reformed church.[1] In 1941, the classis reported that it "strongly disapproves of the continued agitation of the Romig issue, believing that the matter has been satisfactorily explained in our Church paper." What was at issue? Edgar Romig, pastor of the West End Collegiate Church in New York City, had just served as president of the General Synod. In his President's Report to the Synod, he had included a paragraph on the revision of the church's liturgy. The passage concluded with the following sentences:

Traditionalist that I am, I could no more in the Baptism Office ask parents to subscribe to the question, 'Do you believe that our children are sinful and guilty before God?' than I could ask them to believe in Mohammed. For I cannot find warrant in Scripture for any doctrine that children whose wills have not yet been formed and who therefore cannot exercise the power of moral choice are guilty before God.

Those words raised a storm of protest in the church, especially in the western synods of the Reformed church. Several overtures came before the next General Synod, and a number of articles appeared in the *Intelligencer-Leader*. The question engendered sufficient heat to motivate the editor of that paper to travel to New York City to hear Romig's clarification.

Romig told the writer that he was doing nothing more than to ask for a clarity of language in the liturgy that lay persons could understand. The issue was not original sin, Romig argued, but the question of guilt. Could the infant be guilty? Romig answered no. The child hadn't done anything to be guilty of. He then wrote a further clarification for the *Intelligencer-Leader*.

If we were engaged in conversation the writer might be able to bring himself to consent to the world *guilt* in a metonymical sense, it having first been demonstrated that, though innocent of personal and wilful mis-doing each child that is born is through the antecedent transgression of its first ancestor proleptically culpable.

No wonder he was looking for language understandable by the lay person!

His explanation sufficed for the classis. But it shows the classis becoming drawn into the first of a series of theological differences that will divide the denomination east and west.[2]

A similar battle flared later in the same decade at the installation of Hugh Baillie MacLean as president of New Brunswick Seminary. A lively debate among various correspondents to the *Church Herald* (successor to the *Intelligencer-Leader*) had reacted to MacLean's inaugural lecture, which had subsequently been published in the *Herald*. He had boldly embraced a historical-critical approach to Scripture. His lecture included these (apparently) troublesome remarks:

Our minds and consciences today revolt at the wanton destruction attributed, for example, to Joshua and his conquest of the Promised Land. But the explanation lies in the date of these conquest narratives and the background against which they were written. As the Deuteronomic writers saw the picture at the end of the seventh century B.C. with the northern kingdom of Israel in exile and the southern kingdom threatened with imminent destruction, they concluded that the root cause was the secularization of life and religion through contact with the local inhabitants of Canaan. Thus they rewrote the history of Israel with this philosophy in mind.

MacLean's remarks challenged a notion of inspiration dear to many.

The matter came to the floor of the classis, where an extended discussion on the *Church Herald* was held. The classis made no comment on the content of MacLean's lecture. Instead it remarked on the "weakness of human nature...to criticize individuals and institutions with which one is not well acquainted." The classis then claimed that it was "well acquainted" with the program of New Brunswick Theological Seminary, and it sent a letter to MacLean congratulating him and his faculty for "excellent work being accomplished and to commend the Board of Directors and the Board of Superintendents for the high caliber of men added to the teaching staff."[3] This was a glancing rebuke to those who had criticized MacLean.

Church Union

The question of union with Presbyterians of one denomination or another raised itself again during this period as it had occasionally throughout most of the history of the Reformed Church in America. In 1945, the General Synod began mutual conversation with the United Presbyterian church on organic union. By September, 1946, a Plan of Union was to be sent to classes and presbyteries. The synod encouraged fraternal exchanges between the two denominations.[4]

Wasting little time, on September 7, 1946, the classis invited the Presbytery of Albany to a joint meeting on October 1. At that meeting, the two bodies jointly celebrated the Lord's Supper. The presidents of both bodies addressed the gathered assembly.[5]

The matter was important to the classis, and it discussed the union for several years. In March, 1949, it held a special meeting solely to discuss the union. No vote was taken.[6] The following month, the classis formed a Committee on Church Union. At that meeting the classis took a straw vote to ascertain the sense of the classis. Twenty-two votes were cast. Five favored union, three opposed, and fourteen remained undecided.[7]

In 1949, the General Synod instructed the classes to vote after January 1, 1950. Approval of union would require a three-quarter majority in each classis and a three-quarter majority of the classes. Albany Classis voted in April, 1950. The tally read nineteen in favor and seven opposed, a result just short of the seventy-five percent requirement.[8] The union failed across the denomination, having received a bare majority approval. It also failed to receive a favorable vote in the United Presbyterian Church.

The classis was not finished with the idea, however. In 1958, it overtured the General Synod to study merger with the Presbyterians. The synod's Committee on Approaches to Unity recommended no action: "At the present time it would make for greater dissension and disunity within our Church and might occasion possible defection from the Church."[9]

Thus, by 1969, when union with the Presbyterian Church in the United States (the "Southern Presbyterians") was before the Reformed church, the classis stood ready to vote favorably. Indeed, this time an overwhelming majority of thirty-one approved and only four voted against full organic union.[10] Following the defeat of the union in the denomination, the classis resolved to "look forward to the possibility of closer cooperation with the Presbytery of Albany."[11] The dream of church union died hard.

The classis's ecumenical commitment evidenced itself not only in its discussions on church union. The councils of churches were also coming under fire during this period. In 1948, at least one

classis had overtured the General Synod for withdrawal from the
Federal Council of Churches (the predecessor body to the
National Council of Churches). At its 1948 meeting, the synod
had before it a minority report from a special committee to study
the FCC and the National Association of Evangelicals. That report
recommended that the Reformed church sever relations with the
FCC. In a recorded vote, the synod denied the recommendation,
with sixty-five in favor and 150 opposed to withdrawing from the
FCC.

The Classis of Albany stood firmly behind the Reformed
church's continued involvement in the FCC. It overtured the
General Synod that the Reformed church "continue to bear
witness to its oneness with the Protestant denominations of our
country" and that the synod continue its membership in and
support of the FCC.[12]

Locally, the classis became a member of the local council of
churches, the Capital Area Council of Churches, sending
delegates to its board. Later still, in 1971, it joined with the
neighboring classes of Schenectady and Saratoga in becoming a
part of Christians United in Mission, a local ecumenical agency
that included not only Protestant, but significant Roman Catholic
participation.[13]

The Classis as Social Activist

In the controversies surrounding Romig and McLean, and in
the debates over church union, the classis entered a more
assertive period in its life. Still, the classis *reacted* more often
than it initiated. In its social concerns as well, it might be argued
that the classis reacted to events around itself. However, it would
largely initiate its own response, or at least place its own signature
on denominational policies.

Some of its social concerns bespoke long-standing consensus in
the classis. For example, it responded negatively to initiatives to
legalize gambling in New York State. In 1957, the classis went on
record as "strongly opposed" to a move to legalize bingo in the
state. The classis reasoned that stewardship demands that citizens
support worthy projects in a community, without having to rely on
gaming; that the returns achieved in gaming would be eaten up by

overhead; and that gaming is a blight on the legitimate business and moral interests of a community.[14] A decade later, in 1966, the classis "formally" adopted a statement condemning gambling in general and state lotteries in particular.[15] Neither resolution achieved the desired results.

Likewise, the classis continued its opposition to moves that violated the sabbath. However, when it declared its disapproval of business on Sunday in 1965, it added a new twist. In a nod to its newly emboldened ecumenical commitments, it voted to ask the Capital Area Council of Churches and the Roman Catholic diocese to join in its opposition. Further, in a move from the floor of the classis, it charged itself with the task of asking the council of churches to confer not only with the Catholics, but with local labor unions that might be affected by Sunday business.[16]

Other newer issues were also coming to the fore. Race, for example, began to move to the center of concern. Already in 1949, the classis expressed itself on the South African policy of racial separation. It would request General Synod's Committee on Social Welfare

> to give consideration to the condition of racial tension in South Africa and the stand which our Reformed Church in America should take in view of the unfortunate stand of the Dutch Reformed Church in South Africa, since this matter affects our missionary program in India most vitally.

The synod minutes of 1949 show no record of having received this communication. In 1950, on an overture from the classis of Ulster requesting it to communicate its "firm expression of regret" to the Dutch Reformed Church in South Africa, the synod sent greetings to that church, expressing its concern: "We deplore the principle of segregation where ever it is practiced, especially in our own country....Let us never forget that in Christ there is neither Jew nor Gentile, bond nor free."[17]

The classis also examined the issue closer to home. In 1945, Fourth and Fifth (Holland) churches had merged to form Bethany. By 1953 the merged congregation had moved to its present site on New Scotland Avenue, leaving the south end of Albany (a neighborhood on the lower end of the socioeconomic scale). That left the classis with open buildings. At a meeting in 1953, the classis discussed "conducting work among the colored people in the South end of Albany." The president appointed a committee to secure funds to purchase Bethany's building on Schuyler Street (in the south end) for that purpose. The initiative was short-lived, however, and the classis voted permission to sell the building to an AME church. That deal fell through, and the following year the building was sold to Mt. Zion Baptist Church.[18]

Ten years later the classis took up questions of race afresh. This time it was to adopt the denomination's Covenant on Open Occupancy. The Reformed church statement opposed racially restricted housing covenants. But Albany's classis saw particular application in its own backyard. So it added:

...inasmuch as there is in the city of Albany and its surrounding suburbs, a serious problem of segregation in housing, we the members of the Classis of Albany do hereby promise:

1. To resist any attempt on the part of anyone to solicit support for any agreement that would do violence to [the Covenant on Open Occupancy], or any attempt to create an atmosphere of panic and fear.

2. To support one another with all the means possible in our effort to eliminate race as a factor in determining a person's right to make his home in our community.

3. To declare to our neighbors our conviction, giving them every assurance that we desire the continued stability and welfare of our community, that as we would welcome new residents of good character regardless of race, religion, or national origin, so if we would move we would sell only to those of reputable character; and that we believe through avoiding "panic selling" the normal operations within the economic structure of our society will assure us of a stable basis upon which the welfare of our neighborhood might be maintained.

The classis then requested each of its consistories to take similar action. It also voted to send its statement to the newspapers.[19]

Race remained an issue when, in 1968, the classis resolved to "support and encourage" the local chapter of the National Association for the Advancement of Colored People, especially in its attempts to ameliorate the "conditions of Ghetto living" and to further understanding between Albany's city administration and the "Ghetto dwellers."[20] Later the same year, in the heat of a national election campaign, the classis took the unprecedented action of advising the members of its churches to vote. Recalling that in the Humphrey/Nixon presidential campaign, many remarked that the options presented little choice, the classis admonished that "the excuse a failure to vote on the notion that there is no choice is an abdication of the responsibility of the Christian to study the issues, the past records of the candidates, and their proposed programs." But it added a comment on the racial politics of the moment: "to consider seriously whether a vote for George Wallace is consistent with Christian concern for the well being of all the people of our country." For, reasoned the classis, Wallace showed a clear lack of compassion for minority groups. The classis was dismayed at the support for Wallace evidenced among the churches.[21]

The classis also inserted itself into debates local and national around a variety of other issues. In 1964, it reacted to attempts to curb a special state investigation of corruption in local politics surrounding the Ann Lee Home (a county home for the aged). It expressed "disgust and revulsion" at attempts to hamper the investigation and requested the governor to appoint a special prosecutor. In its resolution, the classis prayed that "the people of Albany County arouse themselves from the long night of shameful apathy to a new sense of responsibility and concern from [sic] the welfare of the aged and all the people...."[22]

The classis also went on record favoring a liberalization of New York State divorce laws in 1965. At the same time, in agreement with the New York State Council of Churches, it advocated "medically approved and morally acceptable methods of family planning."[23] It passed a resolution that "publicly favors the repeal of the present laws governing abortion, to the end that the needs of the people be served more realistically." The "present laws" made abortion illegal; the classis was advocating the liberalization of abortion law.[24]

Nor was the classis silent when it came to the war that disturbed the nation in the 1960s, Vietnam. In 1967, the classis voted to carry out an "informational" program on the Vietnamese war.[25] By 1970, the classis was ready to go on record opposing that war. The Evangelism Committee (!) brought a recommendation that the classis adopt the action of the Christian Action Commission of the General Synod. That action had urged a cease-fire from the U.S. side and the beginning of a phased withdrawal of U.S. troops from Vietnam. The classis refused to sign on. The synod's action was not its own action. Instead, it acted to affirm that "the war in Vietnam long has been discredited and is not only odious to us as Christians but contributes mightily to the general malaise of our present urban society."[26]

The classis was acting as a body of churches, mediating an ecclesiastical response to several issues. It was not the congregation, but acted as a gathered body in the particular locality of Albany. Indeed, one can detect the classis's concern for its own urban environment. It mediated several policies of the General Synod to the reality it faced in the local ministry of its own churches.

One other concern, less volatile but none the less crucial, found its place on the classis's agenda. In fact, it kept its place before the classis as other, more immediate, social concerns faded. How were the aged to find homes? Already in 1948, the classis overtured the General Synod to establish homes for the aged in various sections of the denomination. Little came of the initiative at the General Synod level, except that the synod reported the offer of the former home of Helen Gould Shepherd of Roxbury, New York. That home later became Kirkside, a facility originally established to house retired pastors.[27]

Three years later, in 1951, a member of the classis "spoke at length" of the offer of a house in Selkirk to be used as a "Reformed Home for the Aged." Several members commented on the need. But the classis wasn't sure how to finance such a venture. The "Classis voiced its sympathy for the project but felt the entire matter should be carefully studied."[28]

The issue of aging would return with more force in 1971 when the classis endorsed the notion of a Commission on Aging for the five eastern classes in the Synod of Albany. The commission would engage in a feasibility study and would report each step to the classis.[29] The commission became a reality and soon reported that the greatest need for aging people in the Albany area was housing.[30] Again, little came of the effort, and, by 1975, the commission had disbanded. It argued that the five-classis organization was too cumbersome to accomplish the task.[31]

The Classis as Bishop

The classis could not concern itself only with issues that troubled the denomination, nor with social issues that tore at the fabric of the society where it found itself. It had its primary task to which to attend. One of its committees was admonished: "The classis needs to be reminded of its Episcopal function under the constitution of the Reformed Church, and where this can be used to the help and advancement within the bounds of Classis, that it be employed."[32]

Some of its concerns were matters that had troubled the classis from the outset. For example, in his annual Report on the State of Religion in 1966, David Boyce raised the issue of evangelism, of the need of pastors for support, and the lack of supervision of the churches. He spent some energy writing to all the other classes to determine how they exercised supervision and went on to propose that the classis set up a system of visitation of the churches by teams consisting of one pastor and one elder.[33] This sounds little different from discussions held early in the nineteenth century.

The classis continued to be concerned about its ministers. In 1950, it would adopt the first minimum salary guideline. Each church was required to pay its pastor $2,500 per year plus use of a parsonage.[34] The classis would continue to monitor the salaries of its pastors, from time to time raising the "minimum."

It was also kept a close eye on *who* could be called to its pulpits. Echoing a past century, the classis reexamined its policy regarding calling non-Reformed clergy to its pulpits. In 1955, it acted to require that all non-Reformed candidates be interviewed by a committee of three persons to determine his (and it was still "his") spiritual, theological, scholastic, and practical abilities. The candidate could not receive a "promise of a call" until the committee had approved his candidacy. A consistory could appeal a negative report to the entire classis. The classis noted that this was not an official examination as required for ordination.[35]

Thus when, in 1962, the Unionville and New Salem churches desired to place a call upon William Boehne, the classis hesitated. The Church Supervision Committee reported that Boehne was unfamiliar with the doctrinal standards of the Reformed church. It recommended that the churches could employ Boehne for one year as stated supply, during which time a minister from the classis would instruct him in Reformed Standards of Unity and work. The classis did not accept the proposal and voted instead to examine Boehne. The classis records no examination, and within six months Unionville and New Salem called another minister.[36]

The classis not only kept close account of who was in its pulpits; it kept close track of its own ministers. How could it maintain supervision over ministers who were not installed? In 1969, it set up its first formal procedure for its non-installed ministers to report to the classis. If the minister attended at least two classis meetings per year (by the 1960s the classis was meeting four times a year), he was to meet with a team from the classis. If he attended fewer meetings, he was to submit an annual report. A minister engaged in study was required to report annually his course of study, the reasons for the course of study, his intentions following study, and the name and address of the dean of the institution where he was studying. Retired ministers were no less required to submit an annual report if they were not in attendance at classis meetings. However, the classis detailed an official visitor to correspond with or visit all retirees annually.[37]

Nor was the classis's concern for ministry limited to members on its rolls. It engaged in a spirited debate on the nature of ministry itself. In 1958, it held a special session to discuss changes in the Reformed church Constitution centered on ministry. In question was a change that denoted certain ministers as "assistant" as opposed to "associate" ministers. Associates were called to a ministry and installed into a church. Assistants were hired under contractual arrangements and were not installed. The classis hesitated over the lack of security for assistants and voted five for and five against the idea of assistant ministers.[38]

A decade and a half later, the classis hesitated again to accept a fundamental change in the notion of ministry. The General Synod proposed that ministry was no longer to be defined by "office," but by "function." The major change was outlined in a sentence to be added to the preamble of the *Book of Church Order*: "...the three offices which the Reformed Church deems necessary for her ordering are understood to be *essentially functional* in nature, and the term office is everywhere viewed in terms of service rather than of status" [emphasis added]. The classis refused to accept the change in 1972 (nor was the change accepted by the required majority of the classes). However, by 1974, the classis was ready to concede the change.[39]

The classis also exercised its episcopal function in church extension. Actually, "church extension" is most likely a misnomer for the period under view. Something more like realignment began to take place as the population moved to the suburbs.

As early as 1944, the classis's Committee on Church Extension reflected on "non-church areas," a result of population shifts. It promised to survey the area and report its findings.[40] Little was done. Meanwhile, as noted above, Fourth and Fifth merged and moved uptown in Albany to the New Scotland area. Two decades later the president of the classis reported a request from the Albany city churches to the Board of North American Missions asking them to provide a professional consultant to study the problems of the churches in the city.[41] By 1967, Sixth was in serious financial trouble, and the classis worked out a financial arrangement by which the particular synod and the Board of North American Missions would be asked for help. The classis would assess its churches at thirty cents per member to help Sixth.[42] It didn't help. By 1970, Sixth and Bethany jointly requested permission to merge.[43]

Meanwhile, the classis started two churches in its suburban environs. In 1956, Theodore Luidens, pastor of First, Bethlehem, approached the classis about organizing a church in the Glenmont area. The classis requested its Committee on Church Extension and C. A. Dykhuizen, the field secretary of the particular synod, to "survey the field." They reported that land had been given and that favorable conditions prevailed. In September, 1957, the president of the Glenmont Chapel Association asked to have the chapel organized as a church. The classis replied that it needed more time, and it voted to visit the site. Within two weeks, it voted to organize the Glenmont church. The classis also agreed to assess its churches at seventy cents per member to finance the new church's first mortgage.[44]

Seven years later, in 1964, the classis entered a plan to act jointly with First Church in Albany to start a new church in Colonie. A financial plan to support the new church was presented to the classis. It showed First Albany contributing $3,500, while the Board of North American Missions would add $3,200, the Synod of Albany $1,500, and the classis an additional $1,500. However, the classis deleted the phrase that it was acting jointly with First, Albany, and the budget finally approved does not include monies from First.[45]

Thus the classis established its first churches since the turn of the century, and both became suburban churches. However, in neither case, did the classis do the major work of preparation. In the one instance the pastor of First, Bethlehem (the immediate neighbor of the Glenmont church), did the lion's share of the preparation. In the other First, Albany, provided the energy.

The classis acted as bishop more actively concerning liturgical matters. In 1941, it overtured the General Synod to adopt an alternate form for the administration of the Lord's Supper "which may be used permissively." The synod did not act on the request, judging that "the present abridged form" was allowed for the private administration of the sacrament and could be read in about fifteen minutes.[46]

In the turbulent 1960s the classis again addressed liturgical practice. In 1963, the classis established a committee to examine "customs and usages." At immediate issue were questions of baptism, communion, and marriage. Baptism became an issue as the classis asked itself how to interpret the requirement that one parent be a confessing Christian, the role of elders in baptism, and which ministers were permitted to baptize within one of its churches. Communion became a problem when celebrated at conferences and retreats. What minister could celebrate? Who could participate? Was there not a need for elders to be present? Marriage presented the question of the extent and quality of premarital counseling within the classis. The classis wondered: should it set standards for guidance? The classis would overture the General Synod requesting a manual that set out the Reformed position on sacraments, especially baptism. The synod responded that no action was necessary; the curricular materials in the new

Covenant Life Curriculum were sufficient.[47]

By 1966, the classis had a Committee on Liturgy in place. It would answer the question of the celebration of the Supper at retreats, conferences, and the like. The committee agreed that liturgical renewal was returning the sacraments to their central place as a mark of the church; that the sacraments were a symbol of the unity of the church; and that small group experiences provided more personal experiences with the sacrament. Therefore, the classis agreed that members of its churches could participate at times other than those observed by the local congregation. However, certain conditions needed to obtain. The celebrant must be ordained; the "liturgy for the sacrament" must be read; the "constitutional question" must be asked; and one elder needs to be present to answer the question, or if that was not possible, a minister of the Word could answer.[48]

These classis actions can be understood to be part of a more general movement toward liturgical renewal. A new liturgy for the Reformed church was in preparation. Thus, at one meeting the Committee on Liturgy reported a recommendation for the printing of the Gloria, the Agnus Dei, and the Sursum Corda for optional use in the Order for the Lord's Supper. The classis approved the proposal "only after serious consideration."[49] This was strong liturgical medicine for a mildly evangelical denomination. In fact, the classis found it necessary to remind its churches that the orders for the Lord's Supper and Baptism were obligatory, even as it recommended the use of the full liturgy for worship.[50]

A Change in Character

If the period from the 1940s to the 1970s displayed the classis as more involved in controversy, perhaps a more contentious body, a quieter, but more fundamental change was also occurring. The classis had understood itself as "bishop." A bishop concerns himself with establishing and nurturing churches, with the clergy within his "diocese," and with questions of doctrine and worship, all of which concerned the classis most intimately. However, the classis began to stretch its self-understanding beyond a particularly episcopal role. It began to view itself as an agency that provides an array of programs for the churches and members within its bounds. In 1970, the classis established a joint committee with the then Classis of Saratoga to explore merger (a process that culminated in 1978 when the Saratoga Classis was disbanded and several of its larger churches transferred to Albany's classis). The classis stated as the underlying philosophy guiding merger discussions: "The primary purpose of a Classis is to assist and enable the mission of its local congregations by coordinating and pooling the resources of its member churches." The classis was to act as a "resource" for its member congregations. It no longer understood itself to be a public expression of those churches gathered from a local geography. Furthermore, among the reasons given for the merger was the possibility that a larger classis would "allow for more efficient and effective use of personnel resources within classis in fulfilling committee responsibilities both in areas of administration and program." The classis hesitated to adopt the merger. Some members weren't certain that a larger classis would not mean a loss of intimacy. But the classis itself acted to instruct the joint committee to expand its field and to meet with Schenectady Classis (another adjoining body) to "work on a development and sharing of programs." The classis understood itself as a provider of programs.[51]

Much of the impetus came from dynamics at work in the greater church. Craig Dykstra and James Hudnut-Beumler argue that well into the middle of the twentieth century, denominations operated on the model of a corporation that "managed to deliver an incredible array of goods and services...."[52] They write about denominations, not local assemblies and judicatories, but the pressure was felt at a classical level. Furthermore, in 1968, the General Synod brought its various boards under one agency, the General Program Council. What had been a denomination characterized by semiautonomous boards became centralized. The denomination organized to "deliver goods and services." Not long thereafter, following the convulsions of the late 1960s, the denomination "decentralized," locating offices in various regions of the country. The particular synods also began to develop program resources. The classis was the next-lower body, closest to the local congregations. Wasn't it, too, to deliver program?

One detects the move to a more program-centered classis early in the 1960s. At one meeting, for example, the classis reported holding both a classis-wide "mission festival" and a "Classical hymn-sing." Its youth agent announced that the classis would hold a youth conference at Camp Fowler and planned a youth rally for the fall. A newly initiated Committee on Stewardship set up a Stewardship Emphasis Sunday, which included a pulpit exchange among the churches at which the preachers were to preach on the theological basis for stewardship. At the same meeting, the classis resolved to conduct an "elders training course." Evidently the calendar for programs was getting crowded, because the classis charged its Executive Committee to coordinate the course (to be the responsibility of the Men's Brotherhood of the classis) "so as to avoid conflict with other Classis programs and the spring school of theology."[53]

Programs were to proliferate well into the 1970s and included conferences for teacher training, men's retreats, and even a coffee house at Sixth, Albany. The classis even initiated a biannual newsletter for a couple of years.[54] In part, these programs were included to assist the local churches overcome difficulties in their ministries. In response to the concern expressed by one president on flagging youth programs, for example, the classis voted to have its Nurture Committee run a leadership conference for youth leaders.[55] In part, the classis responded to long held concerns. For example, the call to evangelism was repeated several times during this period. One of its committees recommended an evangelistic "crusade" for the classis. The classis didn't go along with the idea, but instead desired to implement a workshop of "at least five sessions" with practical helps in "leading another person to know Christ as his Savior and Lord."[56] In part, as well, Classical programs acted as a bridge between the denomination and the local congregations. In 1975, the classis instructed its Outreach Committee to explore a "mini-mission festival" that "help for Pastors both in administration and communication would overcome some of the problems in RCA emphasis and mission."[57]

By the mid-1970s, however, the classis was beginning to doubt the efficacy of its life as a body that produced programs. In 1976, its Christian Nurture Committee reported that it had cancelled the "School of Religion" because it had too few registrants.[58] It was during the 1960s and 1970s that the classis held an annual

Classical Conference. Its February meeting was given over largely to hearing the president's Report on the State of Religion, and then the classis broke up into workshops. By 1977, the Executive Committee was reporting that it was re-evaluating the annual conference, and within a couple of years, it faded into history.[59]

Underlying the shift to program was an accompanying shift in the structure of the classis itself. In becoming more active, the classis had, in 1960, begun to meet four times each year. A more telling move was the election of a president to serve for a year. Previously, the president was elected each meeting, but the changing organization required a more stable executive.

The classis was becoming more efficient in other ways as well. Not only did it need a stronger executive, but a stronger executive *committee*. Thus, in 1963, it changed its rules of order to require that committee to meet prior to every meeting of the classis. It also began to require that all reports from committees and agents be mailed to the ministers (in duplicate so that elder delegates could receive the reports as well) prior to classis meetings.[60] In fact, the classis restructured itself several times in the 1960s and 70s.

As already noted, this restructuring occurred in response to what was going on in the higher assemblies (there is no mention of a need arising from complaints from the congregations!). One president's report spoke of "centers," denominational offices located in local regions. In the same breath, the president applauded pending new rules of order for the classis: "...these new rules of order will help to make Classis more able to act freely and intelligently, more able to make better-reasoned opinions, better equipped to help the local congregations."[61]

But something was coming apart, too. The same president a year earlier commented that the classis needed a better connection to the new denominational structures. He complained that the congregations had "turned inward."[62] He only echoed concerns voiced a year earlier by his predecessor. That president reflected the worry that funds weren't coming in for "475" (the denominational headquarters), and that educational programs were breaking down on a national level. He met with the chairmen of the various committees of the classis, who agreed that the problem was communication between the classis and the denomination as well as between the classis and its congregations.[63] The unspoken assumption behind these worries was that the classis should "deliver...goods and services." Furthermore, to appeal to "communication" as the problem, is simply to tinker with the structure. It is to assume that the programs offered by the denomination and classis are worthy; the only problem is ignorance at the local level.

What then was the classis to be? In 1973, the president of the classis worried that the particular synod assumed more and more program responsibilities: "this leaves in question what programming will be done on a Classical level." Will the churches "bypass the jurisdiction of the Classis?" Classis responded by asking its committees to clarify their roles with respect to the Synod of Albany. Later the same year, the Executive Committee reported that it "feels that the lines of communication must be open so that the classis is aware of the working of the Synod and is concerned that jurisdictional lines and prerogative be maintained."[64] Again the issue is "communication." But the classis expressed frustration as well. A couple of years later, it spent some time discussing the relation between the classis and the synod and "the obligations pressed on Classis by Synod."[65]

Thus, following 200 years of life, changes in the ecclesiastical landscape left the classis confused as to its role. The question persists. Just what is a classis? Is it to provide programs for its congregations? Is it to deliver the "product" produced by the denomination, or even the local synod? Or is it, rather, to act as "bishop"?

Or can it be argued that the role outlined by the Church Order of Dordt and the Explanatory Articles, and as it began to develop in the early nineteenth century, not only served the classis well, but will continue to do so? As this study turns to the case of the ordination of women, it will show the Classis of Albany in deep historical continuity with the best of its history.

IX
The Ordination of Women:
A Case Study

On a blistering July afternoon in 1979, members of Albany Classis squeezed past the crowd in the Delmar church. With bulletins waving to provide some relief from the heat, the classis ordained Joyce Borgman de Velder to the office of minister of the Word. The classis was doing what it had been in the business of doing from (almost) the beginning. This was different, however. This time, it ordained a woman. This was not the first woman to be ordained to the office of minister of the Word in the Reformed church, but the classis participated in a series of events that effected the acceptance of the legality of the ordination of women in the RCA.

The story of de Velder's ordination is exciting in its own right. It is also a fitting (provisional) conclusion to the story of Albany's classis because it highlights many of the themes that have run through the classis's story. It shows the church not only as congregation or as denomination, but the church as a gathered local body coming to terms with a difficult issue. The classis is about the same business it was about in its beginning—supervision of clergy. It took on the issue with a sort of clumsiness inherent when deliberative bodies must come to conclusion. It was joining the ecumenical consensus on women's ordination, but with its own slowness and reserve. Finally, it acted as that institution that mediated between the local and the national churches.

Indeed, at issue in de Velder's ordination was less the vexing question of whether the church should ordain women than the nature of the polity of the church. Of course, for many folk, the problem was the ordination of women. For some it was high time the church got around to ordaining women, while for others the church most definitely should at least refrain. For many in the Reformed church, Scripture expressly forbade the step. Thus, the issue turned on the authority of Scripture. However, even one noted opponent of women's ordination circulated an essay following the ordination of another female candidate, Joyce Stedge, claiming that he did not contend women's ordination as such, but rather the breach of what he considered to be "constitutional procedures."[1] The classis, to the contrary, will argue for its prerogative as a classis. Late twentieth century Reformed folk were no less passionate about church order than were their forebears.

The Denominational Context

The question of the ordination of women to the office of minister of the Word had circulated in the Reformed church since the mid-1950s. Furthermore, as early as 1918 the Particular Synod of Albany had overtured the General Synod to open the offices of elders and deacons by deleting the word "male" from the requirements for those offices. That request was to return to the General Synod regularly into the middle of the century. The response from the synod remained consistent: the church is not yet ready for such a change. To propose the opening of the offices would provoke dissension in the church. Finally in 1952, the synod upon receipt of thirteen overtures on the matter (six supporting opening the offices to women, and seven opposing it), sent to the classes a proposed amendment deleting the word "male" from the relevant article in the Constitution. Albany's classis supported the change, but it was to be rejected by the classes.[2]

In the meantime, the American Association of Woman Preachers had petitioned the synod in 1942 to receive women as ministers of equivalent ecclesiastical status as men. The synod responded with words of praise for the work women were doing both denominationally and in local congregations. However, since the office of elder had not yet been opened to women, the synod could only reply to the communication in the negative.[3]

Following the negative vote in 1952-53, the synod formed a Committee on the Ordination of Women. By 1956, it was presenting progress reports, and in the following year it presented a series of detailed studies on the issue. This process culminated in 1958 with the synod's "declarative statement": "Scripture nowhere excludes women from eligibility to the offices but always emphasizes their inclusion, prominence, and equal status with men in the Church of Jesus Christ."[4] The synod then sent to the classes once again the proposal that the "offices in the Reformed Church in America shall be open to women and men alike by the year 1962."

Albany Classis again voted in favor of the proposal, but it was to be defeated by the classes. The issue, however, would not go away. By 1964, the General Synod again had an overture requesting an amendment to the Constitution to permit the ordination of women, but it was not until 1971 that the synod proposed a change that would be adopted by the classes. This time the change allowed for the election of elders and deacons from among the entire membership of a local congregation.

Across the denomination, events began to move on two fronts. Throughout the 1970s, the synod repeatedly voted for a change in the Constitution, and repeatedly the change failed to achieve the required two-thirds vote of the classes for ratification. The vote grew ever narrower, however, until in 1975, the vote of the classes registered at twenty-nine in favor, sixteen opposed, and one classis tied in its vote. By this time, many across the church opined that the Constitution *already* allowed for the ordination of women to ministry. As had been often noted, the *Book of Church Order* nowhere required that a candidate for ordination be male. It was assumed that tradition disallowed it, in that the notion of women in ministry had been inconceivable in the earlier recensions of the Constitution. However, many classes agreed to vote on the change for the sake of harmony within the church.

Meanwhile, in 1973, Joyce Stedge, a graduate of Union Seminary in New York and under the care of the Rockland-Westchester Classis, came under consideration by the General Synod for a dispensation from the professorial certificate. The Board of Theological Education, the synod's agent to recommend such matters, had recommended approval of Rockland-

Westchester's request on her behalf. The recommendation brought confusion and consternation on the floor of the General Synod, and a ruling was requested from the chair. How could this be? The president, Harry De Bruyn, ruled that both the application and the recommendation were within the provisions of the *Book of Church Order*. The ruling was appealed to the floor of the synod, but the appeal lost.[5] This vote neither approved the ordination of women, nor the ordination of Joyce Stedge. However, the Classis of Rockland-Westchester, seeing in the Constitution no bar to her ordination, proceeded to ordain her in 1978.

Stedge's ordination and subsequent installation in the Rochester Church in Accord, New York, produced a firestorm of anger across the denomination. By 1974, the synod had received three overtures requesting the synod to declare Stedge's licensure and ordination null and void, and another overture to establish a special committee to study the legality of the president's 1973 ruling and the actions of the classes who licensed, ordained, and installed Stedge. Synod took no action. Furthermore, complaints brought against Rockland-Westchester—a judicial act—were dismissed by the synod. The complainants had no standing to achieve redress; they were not members of the assembly, the classis, that took the action.

Albany's Action

Although the vote to ordain de Velder provided the focal point for the ensuing controversy, Albany Classis had prepared to act prior to her arrival. In June, 1975, Lucille Beagle, a member of First Church in Albany, applied to be taken under the care of the classis and was received. Undoubtedly, the classis had anticipated a change in the Constitution that would allow for the ordination of women to the office of minister of the Word. In fact, in June, 1976, the classis voted to give Beagle the right to candidate and to receive a promise of a call.[6] Repeated votes had shown a decided majority in favor of the change across the denomination, and the majority appeared to be growing.

In fact, the classis itself had long supported changes in the Constitution of the Reformed church designed to open all the offices of the church to women. Already in 1952, it had voted to support the proposed change in the Constitution that dropped the word "male" in the section of the Constitution that limited the offices of elder and deacon to males.[7] As late as 1969, in response to an initiative from First, Bethlehem, the classis proposed a compromise that would make the ordination of women to the offices of elder and deacon a matter of "local option." It requested that General Synod allow each classis to decide the matter for the churches within their respective bounds. If accomplished, women were to constitute no more than twenty-five percent of any consistory.[8] The proposal died a quick death.

Then, in 1977, the Delmar church hired Joyce de Velder as an associate in ministry. She had not been ordained and thus could not be installed in her position. However, she had been licensed by the Classis of Muskegon. This placed her in the anomalous position of being given ecclesiastical authority to accept a call without clear provision that she could be ordained once she received a call! In any case, Albany Classis accepted her under its care February 13, 1977, and the following month she read and signed the Declaration for Licensed Candidates before the classis. Then, in May of the same year, the Vocational Development Committee of the classis (the committee that supervised students for the ministry and their examinations) judged that Lucille Beagle (Kramer) had met the requirements necessary for examination by the classis. The classis examined her and voted to approve her examination for licensure and ordination. The way was paved for another woman to be ordained by the classis.

It was a year before the classis was prepared to consider de Velder's ordination. But in June, 1978, the Vocational Development Committee argued that since de Velder was a fully trained candidate for ministry, that she had passed her examinations for licensure and ordination in the Classis of Muskegon, that she fulfilled all the qualifications for ordination as required by the *Book of Church Order*, and since she was already a licensed candidate engaged in ministry, the classis should ordain her. The committee provided the classis with a rationale:

1. Her ordination would strengthen the mission of Christ through the Reformed church. The ordination would show "that the church continues to speak to a changing age."
2. Her ordination would affirm the Book of Church Order "in which we find sufficient grounds for this ordination."
3. "Theological and biblical studies which show that there is not hindrance to the ordination of women have been approved by the General Synod."
4. Some classes have taken women students under care, examined them, and "consented" to ordain them.
5. The seminaries of the Reformed church receive women as students and continue to grant them professorial certificates.
6. The majority of the classes continue to vote in favor of women's ordination.

As the classis deliberated, it asked itself several questions: Does this person meet the requirements? What will ordination mean for this particular woman? What will the ordination mean for the Reformed church? And what would the consequences be for the classis if it should ordain a woman?

The classis had in hand letters of support for de Velder's ordination both from the consistory of the Delmar Church and from Gerard Van Heest, pastor at Delmar. After extended debate, the classis voted to ordain de Velder. The vote was close; twenty-four voted in favor, fifteen voted against, and eight abstained. The classis appointed a committee to make arrangements for the ordination.[9]

By October, plans for de Velder's ordination were in place. The classis received a motion to set December 3, 1978, as the date. However, events had overtaken the anticipated ordination. Several complaints had been lodged against the action to ordain. Thus, a secondary motion was voted to postpone the ordination until the particular synod had acted on the complaints against the classis.

The Complaint

Several members of the classis, both clergy and elder, complained its action to ordain de Velder. Most were ruled out of order by the particular synod's Overtures and Judicial Business Committee as not conforming to the requirements of the *Book of Church Order*. One complaint, however, was allowed. It was brought by the consistory of the Wynantskill church and was signed by John C. Hintermaier and Robert Roseberger, both elder delegates to the classis from Wynantskill.

The complaint alleged that the classis violated the *Book of Church Order* "only on the grounds that this violates the present General Synod interpretation of the words, 'person and he,' to mean male when applied to those ordained to the Gospel Ministry." However, the Wynantskill complainants offered a rather odd rationale. They argued that they believed that the General Synod's interpretation was wrong, and "ask that...'person and he' be ruled to include both male and female." They went on to request that "a judicial ruling supporting this viewpoint be made by the Particular Synod, and, if necessary, the General Synod, as to the definition of the use of 'person and he' in regard to those ordained to the Gospel Ministry." The complainants, evidently, desired to have the synod rule *against* them while arguing at the same time that the classis had acted out of order.[10]

The particular synod, however, was finding it difficult to resolve the case. The chair of the Committee on Overtures and Judicial Business found it almost impossible to gather a quorum. At one meeting, November 20, 1978, only two members were present, along with counsel and the stated clerk. Working without a quorum, the committee systematically worked through the complaints. Interestingly, at that meeting, the committee was prepared to rule against the Wynantskill complaint.

When the committee convened in early February, 1979, in preparation for the particular synod meeting, only the chair appeared, along with counsel. This was to be a crucial meeting, as the committee was charged by the Constitution to hear the parties to the case. Thus, only the chair heard arguments from Hintermaier and the classis. Almost in desperation, the chair called a meeting for February 17, 1979, on the morning of the synod meeting called to review the complaint. The members were instructed to come prepared to vote and to bring with them statements that would provide a rationale.

On February 17, 1979, the Synod of Albany met at the

Community Reformed Church in Colonie, located between Albany and Schenectady. The classis had prepared a response to the complaint that argued in essence that the classis had acted within a proper understanding of the *Book of Church Order*. However, the synod's Overtures and Judicial Business Committee recommended a ruling against the classis. The majority argued variously that the *Book of Church Order* intended the word "person" to refer to "male"; that the classis offends against the precedent of the denomination; and that the "law of our Church is based on history and precedent."

The recommendation of the committee was to carry the day. A move to reject the report was defeated by one vote. The classis was directed not to ordain de Velder.

The classis, unwilling to give up, quickly filed its intent to complain and to form a committee to draft a complaint to the General Synod. Here, however, the difficulty of a body acting in concert under the pressure of time reveals itself. It had to prepare, debate, and present its complaint within a relatively short period of time.

Albany joined with several other synods and classes in the judicial process. Bergen and Brooklyn classes had both ordained women, and their actions had been upheld by the synods of New Jersey and New York, respectively. Albany's position was different, however. It took the offensive. It could argue that it had been harmed.

Its complaint argued that the particular synod committed several administrative errors, any one of which should cause the decision to be overturned. However, the weight of its argument rested on what it considered to be the prerogatives of the classis. Fundamentally, it argued that with the request to ordain Joyce de Velder, it no longer was debating an issue but was faced with a decision. It is the task of a classis to judge the worthiness of candidates to the office of minister of the Word. The classis could find no bar to her ordination in the qualifications set forth in the Constitution. The only mention of gender came in the pronouns used. A close reading of the *Book of Church Order* had long shown that it had used the term "person" when referring to ministers of the Word. While the Constitution used the male pronoun, the usage could be understood generically. Thus, the classis found no bar to ordination. In fact, given the 1958 "declarative statement" by the General Synod, the classis could do little other than it did. How could it act contrary to what the synod had declared that Holy Scripture taught?

Furthermore, the classis argued that it had the right and responsibility to interpret the *Book of Church Order* in matters that came before it. It was not the purview of the General Synod to rule on abstract cases but only on particular cases that came before it for adjudication. The classis could refer to the General Synod of 1897:

> It is the settled principle of the General Synod, as it is of the Supreme Court of the United States, and nearly all other judicatories, both ecclesiastical and civil, never to adjudicate an abstract question, but to take|cognizance only of concrete cases. In this case Synod is asked for an interpretation of a phrase, or rather, for a definition of a word in the Constitution. This is not the province of Synod. Every Consistory, Classis and Particular Synod is at liberty to interpret the Constitution according to its candid judgment, but the appication of such interpretation is always subject to review.[11]

In effect, the classis argued that no change in the Constitution had been required, and that it was acting by its best judgment.

It argued further that with the removal of the barrier to the ordination of women to the offices of elder and deacon, theologically the office of minister of the Word was open to women as well. It could appeal to a report from the Committee on the Ordination on Women to the General Synod in 1957:...while there are definite distinctions of function, the offices have essentially an identity of nature which makes it impossible to draw a line that is clear and decisive in determining the question of eligibility. In other words, if any office should be opened to women, all of them should be.[12]

More crucially, the classis could cite the Liturgy, itself a part of the Constitution:

> The Reformed Church has maintained these ministries in the offices of the minister of the Word, of the elder, and of the deacon. Since there is a unity of these offices in Christ himself, so also in the Church the one office is not to be

separated from the others.[13]

Opponents to Albany's action pointed out that the continued attempt to amend the *Book of Church Order* and Albany's continued vote for the approval of the change indicated a tacit approval by the classis to the requirement for change. However, Albany's representatives to the General Synod's hearing argued orally that the amendments proposed were little more than "clarifying amendments," a not uncommon action by the church to resolve unnecessary ambiguity in its Constitution.

These arguments carried the day. On Wednesday morning, June 15, 1979, the General Synod met in Hope College's gymnasium to hear the report of its Commission on Judicial Business. However, before anything got started, a delegate asked whether the synod had before it an appeal or a complaint. This apparently abstruse question had a stinger. If the issue were an appeal, then members of the classes or synods involved could not vote. Since fully half of the synods, Albany, New Jersey, and New York, were parties, an appeal would disenfranchise a significant number of delegates. And since it had been clear that support for women's ordination continued to be strongest in those synods and weakest in the three western synods, a ruling that the synod had before it an appeal would most likely end the matter. However, on advice of the general secretary, the chair ruled that the synod had before it a complaint.

The Commission on Judicial Business had met several times to hear the parties and to debate its decision. Its report concluded, following review of the various complaints against the synods of New York and New Jersey and Albany's complaint:

> It is our finding that in each instance the classes interpreted the *Book of Church Order* regarding the ordination of persons in good faith and withoutdefiance; they exercised the prerogatives of the classis in the Reformed Church in following the procedure for care, examination, licensure and ordination of a candidate who has met all the requirements of the *Book of Church Order*.[14]

Thus, the commission judged that "no deliberate, intentional or actual violation of the *Book of Church Order* took place on the part of the classes complained against." The debate on the Commission's recommendations was extended, even heated. But the Albany's complaint was sustained. It could proceed to ordain Joyce de Velder.

Concluding Remarks

This case illustrates a classis acting as a mediating institution. It expressed the judgment not only of the plurality of church members in its congregations, but of the officers, ministers of the Word, and elders, gathered in one place. It argued the matter in larger forums. The issue itself arose from a particular church within its bounds and a particular person who appeared as a candidate for ministry. Furthermore, the case displayed the classis in deliberate argument around matters of scripture and church order. The passion for both shows the classis not so far from its roots in the late eighteenth century as one might expect from its more recent attempts at accommodation to the ecclesiastical frenzy of the late twentieth century.

In fact, the case of women's ordination shows the classis at its strongest point. It could and did function as an institution that sustained both ministers and churches through a trying time and over a period of years. Despite the stresses and strains placed on it by its environment, it continued to adjudicate delicate and difficult issues without breaking apart. It could indeed sustain a way of being a gathered church in its local, trans-parochial expression.

Endnotes

Introduction

1. The story of the church in Albany is ably told by Robert S. Alexander in *Albany's First Church: Its Role in the Growth of the City* (Albany: First Church in Albany, 1988). Alexander is particularly good on the early settlement of Albany and its church.
2. The notable exception is the work of Gerald De Jong on the history of the Classis of Dakota. Some years ago I read De Jong's work in manuscript. It provided much of the inspiration for this study.
3. Maurice G. Hansen, *The Reformed Church in the Netherlands traced from A.D. 1340 to A.D. 1840,* (New York: Board of Publication of the Reformed Church in America, 1884), pp. 83, 84.
4. Alexis De Tocqueville, *Democracy in America*, trans. Henry Reeve (London: Oxford University Press, 1946), p. 304.
5. Nathan O. Hatch, *The Democratization of American Christianity* (New Haven: Yale University Press, 1989), p. 5.
6. "Imposters," *The Lutheran Magazine*, II (December, 1928), p. 265.
7. *The Liturgy of the Reformed Church in America together with The Psalter*, ed. Gerrit T. Vander Lugt (New York: The Board of Education), p. 111.
8. See David G. Hackett, *The Rude Hand of Innovation: Religion and Social Order in Albany, New York 1652-1836* (Oxford: Oxford University Press, 1991) as an illuminating example of this genre. Hackett takes Albany into the nineteenth century.
9. Daniel J. Meeter, *Meeting Each Other: In Doctrine, Liturgy & Government*, The Historical Series of the Reformed Church in America, No. 24 (Grand Rapids: Eerdmans, 1993).

Chapter I

1. Charles E. Corwin, *A Manual of the Reformed Church in America, 5th ed. rev.* (New York: Board of Publication and Bible-School Work of the Reformed Church in America, 1922), p. 263.
2. For a full account of the Coetus-Conferentie dispute see Gerald F. De Jong, *The Dutch Reformed Church in the American Colonies*, The Historical Series of the Reformed Church in America, No. 5 (Grand Rapids: Eerdmans, 1978), pp. 188 ff.
3. *Ecclesiastical Records of the State of New York*, published under the supervision of Hugh Hastings (Albany: J. B. Lyon 1905), vol. VI, p. 4213. Hereinafter noted as "Hastings."
4. Ibid.
5. Ibid., p. 4124.
6. *Minutes of the General Synod*, October 8, 1773. Hereinafter noted as *MGS*.
7. *MGS*, October 6, 1778.
8. Ibid.
9. Hastings, p. 4319.
10. The General Meeting of Ministers and Elders changed the name of "assemblies" to "synods" in October, 1784, noting that "assemblies" had caused "difficulties and inconsistencies." Hastings, p. 4321.
11. *MGS*, October 4, 1785.
12. *MGS*, October 3 1780.
13. *MGS*, October 3, 1786.
14. *MGS*, May 18, 1784.
15. *MGS*, October 4, 1785.
16. Hastings, p. 4383.
17. Minutes of the Classis of Albany, July 30, 1800. Hereinafter noted as "Minutes."
18. Hatch, p. 23.
19. Hackett, p. 69.
20. Minutes, January 20, 1801.
21. MGS, June, 1800.
22. *Minutes of the Particular Synod of Albany*, October 13, 1807. Hereinafter noted "MSA."
23. Minutes, April 28, 1801.
24. *MSA*, May 21, 1801.
25. Minutes, September 27, 1803.
26. *MSA*, June 2, 1802, and October 11, 1808, and Minutes, April 26, 1803 and September 27, 1803.
27. *MSA*, June 2, 1802, and *MGS*, May, 1804.
28. *MSA*, October 10, 1915, *MGS*, 1816, pp. 25-27, and *MGS*, 1817, p. 27
29. Elizabeth D. Shaver, *A Serving People: A History of the Niskayuna Reformed Church* (1966), pp. 20-22.
30. Minutes, September 29, 1801, and February 10, 1802.
31. Alexander, pp. 166ff.
32. Ibid., p. 170.
33. *MSA*, October 31, 1804, October 8, 1805, October 14, 1806, and October 13, 1807.
34. *MGS,* June, 1809, pp. 392-393.
35. *MGS,* June, 1806, p. 357.
36. *MGS,* June, 1809, PP. 388-389.

37. Minutes, September 27, 1803.
38. Minutes, August 18-19, 1818, *MGS*, 1813, *MGS*, 1819, and *MGS*, 1820.
39. *MSA*, June 28, 1803.
40. *MGS*, June 1806, pp. 359-360.
41. The Explanatory Articles required that two Synodical deputies, the "Deputati Synodi," be present at every examination of a candidate for ministry by a classis. Their role was to "see that the examination was performed with strictness, propriety, and justice" (Article 41).

Chapter II

1. Robert McDowall, "Statement of the Rev. Robert McDowall Concerning Early History of Presbyterian Work in Upper Canada, Addressed to the Rev. Henry Gordon. Dated 18th January, 1839," Archives, The Presbyterian Church in Canada, Toronto, Canada; and John S. Moir, "Robert McDowall, Pioneer Dutch Reformed Missionary in Upper Canada," *Presbyterian History: A Newsletter of the Committee On History*, The Presbyterian Church in Canada, vol. 23, nos. 1-3.
2. McDowall.
3. *MSA*, May 20-21, 1801.
4. Ibid.
5. Minutes, April 26, 1803.
6. *MGS*, May, 1804, pp. 331, 340.

7. *MGS*, June, 1806, pp. 352, 353.
8. *Magazine of the Reformed Dutch Church*, vol. I, no. 1, April, 1826.
9. Ibid.
10. *MSA*, October 10, 1809.
11. *MGS*, June, 1812, p. 425.
12. *Magazine of the Reformed Dutch Church*, vol. I, no. 1.
13. *MGS*, June, 1816, pp. 35-36.
14. *MSA*, November 20, 1816.
15. Ibid.
16. *MGS*, June, 1817, pp. 9-14.
17. *MGS*, June, 1818, pp. 34-36.
18. Moir.
19. *MGS*, June, 1820.
20. Moir.

Chapter III

1. Minutes, February 15, 1831.
2. Hatch, pp. 8-9.
3. Ibid., p. 15.
4. Ibid. p. 81.
5. Ibid., p. 63.
6. Ibid., p. 140.
7. Hackett, p. 10.
8. Ibid., p. 49.
9. Ibid., p. 82.
10. Ibid., pp. 98-99.
11. Ibid., pp. 126ff.
12. Ibid., pp. 124, 125.
13. James Van Hoeven, "Dort and Albany: Reformed Theology Engages a New Culture," in *Word and World*, ed. James Van Hoeven, The Historical Series of the Reformed Church in America, No. 16 (Grand Rapids: Eerdmans, 1986), p. 17.

14. James Spencer Cannon, *Lectures in Pastoral Theology* (New York: Charles Scribner, 1853), p. 586.
15. Ibid., p. 588, emphasis in original.
16. Ibid., p. 590, emphasis in original.
17. Ibid., p. 597, emphasis in original.
18. Van Hoeven, pp. 19-20.
19. Ibid.
20. *MGS*, 1814.
21. This is a serious lacuna. The classis's minutes from 1822-1829 are missing.
22. *MSA*, August 18, 1824.
23. Amasa J. Parker, *Landmarks of Albany County* (Syracuse, NY: D. Mason, 1897), p. 497.
24. Corwin, p. 592.
25. Minutes, August 18-19, 1818.
26. *MSA*, May 20, 1823.
27. Minutes, September, 1829.
28. Minutes, February 16, 1830.
29. Minutes, April 17, 1832.
30. Minutes, April 16, 1833.
31. Minutes, April 21, 1840.
32. Minutes, April 18, 1843.
33. Minutes, April 16, 1844.
34. Hatch, pp. 19, 20.
35. Minutes, September, 1829.
36. Minutes, November 10, 1834.
37. Minutes, September 20, 1836.
38. Minutes, February 20, 1835.
39. Minutes, January 26, 1837
40. Minutes, April 21, 1840.
41. Minutes, April 20, 1841.
42. Minutes, November 21, 1833.
43. Minutes, April 18, 1837.
44. Minutes, April 20, 1841.
45. Minutes, November 1, 1842.
46. Minutes of the Consistory of the Jerusalem Reformed Church, March 29, 1851.
47. Minutes, April 15, 1851.
48. Ibid.
49. Ibid.
50. Minutes, April 20, 1841.
51. Minutes, April 16, 1844.
52. Minutes, April 21, 1840.
53. Minutes, April 21, 1846, *MSA*, May 5, 1847.
54. Minutes, February 16, 1830.
55. Minutes, October 28, 1841.
56. Minutes, September 16, 1851.
57. Minutes, April 20, 1841.
58. Minutes, April 19, 1842; November 1, 1842.
59. Minutes, April 19, 1842.
60. Hatch, pp. 170, 171.
61. Minutes, August 15, 1820.
62. Minutes, February 16, 1830.
63. Minutes, April 16, 1833.

Chapter IV

1. Martin E. Marty, *Protestantism in the United States: Righteous Empire*, 2nd ed. (New York: Charles Scribner's, 1986).
2. Ibid., p. 69.
3. Marvin D. Hoff, *Structures for Mission*, The Historical Series of the Reformed Church in America, No. 14 (Grand Rapids: Eerdmans, 1985), pp. 29ff.
4. Ibid., p. 33.
5. Minutes, February 16, 1830.

6. Minutes, September 17, 1850.
7. Minutes, September 18, 1838.
8. Minutes, April 17, 1855.
9. Minutes, November 19, 1856.
10. Minutes, April 16, 1861.
11. MGS, 1862, pp. 189 ff.
12. Minutes, April 15, 1862.
13. Minutes, September 17, 1872.
14. Minutes, September 18, 1866. Emphasis in the original.
15. Ibid.
16. Minutes, April 21, 1875.
17. Minutes, September 18, 1885.
18. Minutes, September 21, 1852.
19. Minutes, November 19, 1856.
20. Minutes, September 18, 1883.
21. Minutes, April 19, 1870.
22. Minutes, September 19, 1893.
23. Minutes, September 17, 1867.
24. Minutes, April 18, 1871.
25. Marty, p. 50.
26. Corwin, p. 453.
27. Minutes, July 8, 1847, December 5, 1848, and September 17, 1850.
28. Minutes, September 17, 1872.
29. Minutes, September 16, 1890.
30. Minutes, April 19, 1881.
31. MGS, October 1, 1793.
32. Minutes, April 27, 1802.
33. Minutes, September, 1839.
34. Minutes, August 21, 1821. Emphasis in original.
35. Minutes, April 16, 1833.
36. Minutes, December 3, 1834.
37. Minutes, September 2, 1842.
38. Minutes, January 3, 1848.
39. Minutes, April 18, 1854.
40. Minutes, October 19, 1854.
41. Minutes, April 15, 1856.
42. John G. Meengs, compiler, Historical Sketch of the Third Reformed Church, Albany, N.Y. (Albany: J.W. Johnson, 1906), p. 14.
43. Minutes, January 24, 1860.
44. Minutes, September, 1846.
45. Minutes, April 20, 1849.
46. Ibid.
47. Minutes, April 18, 1848.
48. Minutes, September 21, 1852.
49. Minutes, April 19, 1853.
50. Minutes, September 20, 1853.
51. Minutes, September 20, 1859.
52. Minutes, September 15, 1867.
53. Minutes, April 16, 1895.
54. Hastings, p. 4369.
55. Minutes, April 26, 1803.
56. Minutes of the Consistory of Fourth Reformed Church of Albany, 1855-1865, Archives of the Reformed Church in America, New Brunswick Theological Seminary, New Brunswick, New Jersey.
57. Minutes, April 17, 1855.
58. Minutes, April 20, 1858.
59. Minutes, April 15, 1862
60. Minutes, April 18, 1876.
61. Minutes, April 15-16, 1902.
62. Minutes, April 21, 1868.
63. Minutes, September 17, 1872.
64. Minutes, April 21, 1885.
65. Minutes, September 21, 1897; and December 21, 1897.
66. Minutes, February 6, 1899.
67. MGS, May 13, 1789.
68. Hackett, pp. 53-55.

69. Minutes, May 15, 1821.
70. Minutes, April 20, 1858.
71. Minutes, April 16, 1844; MGS, 1843, pp. 179-181. "Mercersburg theology" was so named after the seminary of the German Reformed church in Mercersberg, Pennsylvania. John Williamson Nevin, American-born, German-educated, came to Mercersburg in 1840 to be followed in 1844 by the German church historian, Philip Schaff. The two advocated a high understanding of the church and its sacraments and promoted an ecumenical vision. These emphases found few adherents in the Dutch church of the middle eighteenth century.
72. Minutes, April 19, 1887.
73. MGS, 1891, pp. 349-356.
74. Minutes, April 19, 1892; MGS, 1892, pp. 577ff.
75. MGS, 1893, pp. 816ff. Herman Harmelink III, Ecumenism and the Reformed Church, The Historical Series of the Reformed Church in America, No. 1 (Grand Rapids: Eerdmans, 1968), pp. 38-52.
76. Minutes, April 21, 1840.
77. Minutes, April 18, 1865.
78. Minutes, April 20, 1847.
79. Minutes, April 15, 1851.
80. Minutes, September 19, 1848.
81. Minutes, April 18, 1871.
82. Minutes, April 18, 1854; MGS, 1853, pp. 377ff.; MGS, 1854, p. 494.

83. Minutes, September 17, 1867.
84. Minutes, April 21, 1857.
85. Minutes, April 18, 1876.
86. Minutes, September 17, 1861.
87. Minutes, April 15, 1862.
88. Minutes, April 19, 1881.

Chapter V

1. Minutes, September 18, 1855.
2. Minutes, September 16, 1956.
3. Minutes, September 15, 1857.
4. Minutes, April 19, 1881.
5. Ibid.
6. Minutes, April 20, 1875.
7. Minutes, April 16, 1867.
8. These figures can be found in the Minutes of General Synod of different years.
9. Minutes, April 20, 1858.
10. Minutes, April 21, 1868.
11. Minutes, April 20, 1869.
12. Minutes, April 18, 1876.
13. Minutes, April 17, 1877.
14. Minutes, April 15, 1879
15. Minutes, April 18, 1882.
16. Minutes, September 15, 1896.
17. Minutes, September 16, 1856.
18. Minutes, October 30, 1867.
19. Minutes, April 20, 1852.
20. Minutes, April 17, 1883.
21. Minutes, September 20, 1864.
22. Minutes, April 18, 1876.
23. Minutes, September 21, 1880.
24. Minutes, November 17, 1853.
25. Minutes, March 23, 1863.
26. U.S. Department of Commerce, Historical Statistics of the United States: Colonial Times to 1970

(1975), pp. 164, 322.

27. Minutes, April 17, 1894.

28. Minutes, September 16, 1884.

29. Minutes, September 15, 1891.

Chapter VI

1. Martin E. Marty, *Modern American Religion, vol 1: The Irony of It All 1893-1919* (Chicago: The University of Chicago Press, 1986).

2. Minutes, April 16-17, 1901.

3. Minutes, April 17-18, 1900.

4. Minutes, April 21-22, 1903.

5. Minutes, April 16-17, 1901.

6. Minutes, April 17, 1906.

7. *MSA,* May 4, 1909, pp. 11-13.

8. *MGS,* 1892, p. 567.

9. Minutes, April 17, 1917.

10. Minutes, May 13, 1907.

11. Minutes, May 12, 1913.

12. Minutes, April 17, 1917.

13. Minutes, December 10, 1900.

14. Minutes, September 22, 1908.

15. Minutes, June 22, 1910.

16. Minutes, April 16, 1895.

17. Minutes, April 18-19, 1899; September 26, 1899; December 10, 1900; April 15-16, 1902.

18. Minutes, April 17-18, 1900.

19. Minutes, September 24, 1901.

20. Minutes, December 10, 1900.

21. Minutes, September 24, 1901.

22. Minutes, April 15-16, 1902.

23. Minutes, October 13, 1903; October, 31, 1904.

24. Minutes, April 17, 1906.

25. Minutes, April 20, 1915.

26. Minutes, April 19-20, 1904.

27. Minutes, October 21, 1904; November 14, 1904.

28. Minutes, December 11, 1905; April 17, 1906; May 21, 1906.

29. Minutes, September 26, 1911; September 23, 1913.

30. Minutes, February 9, 1903.

31. Minutes, April 21-22, 1903.

32. Minutes, September 22, 1903; October 13, 1903.

33. Minutes, November 2, 1903.

34. Minutes, November 17, 1903; December 8-9, 1903.

35. Minutes, April 19-20, 1904; September 21, 1904; September 26, 1905; June 6, 1906; September 25, 1906; September 28, 1909; September 27, 1910; *MSA,* 1906, pp. 13-15.

36. Minutes, September 24, 1901.

Chapter VII

1. Martin E. Marty, *Modern American Religion, vol. 2: The Noise of Conflict* (Chicago: The University of Chicago Press, 1991).

2. Ibid., pp. 15-16.

3. Ibid., p. 22.

4. Minutes, April 15, 1919.

5. Minutes, April 20, 1920.

6. Mildred W. Schuppert, *A Digest and Index of the Minutes of the General Synod of the Reformed Church in America, 1906-1957,* The Historical Series of the Reformed Church in America,

no. 8 (Grand Rapids: Eerdmans, 1982), p. 69.

7. Ibid., p. 209.
8. Minutes, January 22, 1920.
9. Minutes, April 17, 1928.
10. Minutes, October 18, 1927; April 17, 1928; October 16, 1928; April 16, 1929.
11. Minutes, April 18, 1933.
12. Minutes, October 15, 1940.
13. Minutes, October 15, 1929.
14. Minutes, April 19, 1932.
15. Minutes, April 16, 1940.
16. Minutes, April 16, 1929.
17. Minutes, October 20, 1931.
18. Minutes, October 17, 1933.
19. Minutes, April 18, 1933.
20. Minutes, October 18, 1932.
21. Minutes, September 23, 1919.
22. Minutes, April 16, 1929.
23. Minutes, June 30, 1926.
24. Minutes, March 1, 1939.
25. Minutes, March 16, 1932.
26. Minutes, October 21, 1924.
27. Minutes, July 20, 1928; October 16, 1928.
28. Minutes, April 15, 1919.
29. Minutes, April 16, 1929.
30. Minutes, April 20, 1926.
31. Minutes, April 15, 1919.
32. Minutes, April 21, 1931.
33. Minutes, October 16, 1928.
34. Minutes, April 15, 1919.
35. Minutes, April 17, 1923.
36. Minutes, October 16, 1923.
37. Minutes, October 21, 1924.
38. Minutes, April 21, 1925.
39. Marty, *Noise of Conflict*, p. 232.
40. John A. De Jong, "Social

Concerns," in James W. Van Hoeven, *Piety and Patriotism*, The Historical Series of the Reformed Church in America, No. 4 (Grand Rapids: Eerdmans, 1976), pp. 122, 123.
41. Minutes, April 17, 1923.
42. Minutes, April 15, 1930.
43. Minutes, October 20, 1936.

Chapter VIII

1. As in previous wars, the classis had little comment on the war. The churches, of course, were deeply affected. Third, Albany, for example, reported that they had fifty members and twenty-five adherents in "active war service." Minutes, April 18, 1944.
2. Minutes, October 28, 1941; *The Intelligencer-Leader*, June, 13, 1941, p. 7; *The Intelligencer-Leader*, October 3, 1941, p. 5.
3. Minutes, April 19, 1949; *Church Herald*, October 22, 1948, p. 17.
4. Schuppert, I, p. 263.
5. Minutes, September 9, 1946.
6. Minutes, March 19, 1949.
7. Minutes, April 19, 1949.
8. Minutes, April 18, 1950.
9. Minutes, March 18, 1958
10. Minutes, January 21, 1969.
11. Minutes, June 17, 1969.
12. Minutes, April 20, 1948.
13. Minutes, January 19, 1971.
14. Minutes, October 15, 1957.
15. Minutes, March 15, 1966.
16. Minutes, September 14, 1965.

17. Minutes, April 19, 1949; *MGS*, 1950, p. 312.
18. Minutes, May 24, 1953; March 8, 1954.
19. Minutes, October 15, 1963.
20. Minutes, June 18, 1968.
21. Minutes, October 15, 1968.
22. Minutes, January 21, 1964.
23. Minutes, March 16, 1965.
24. Minutes, January 20, 1970.
25. Minutes, March 14, 1967.
26. Minutes, January 20, 1970.
27. Minutes, April 10, 1948.
28. Minutes, April 17, 1951.
29. Minutes, October 19, 1971.
30. Minutes, June 10, 1972
31. The issue remained. In 1986, beyond the scope of this history, the classis incorporated the Classis of Albany Homes to provide housing for the elderly. After a bold start that included leasing a home for community living, the venture found that few persons availed themselves of the ministry and the initiative became dormant once again.
32. Minutes, October 18, 1949.
33. Minutes, March 15, 1966.
34. Minutes, October 17, 1950.
35. Minutes, April 19, 1955.
36. Minutes, January 16, 1962.
37. Minutes, March 18, 1962.
38. Minutes, March 31, 1948.
39. Minutes, January 18, 1972; March 19, 1974.
40. Minutes, October 17, 1944.
41. Minutes, September 30, 1963.
42. Minutes, March 14, 1967.
43. Minutes, June 16, 1970.
44. Minutes, May 29, 1956; September 12, 1957; September 26, 1957.
45. Minutes, October 20, 1964; January 19, 1965.
46. Minutes, April 21, 1941; *MGS*, 1941, pp. 143-144.
47. Minutes, October 15, 1963.
48. Minutes, January 18, 1966.
49. Minutes, January 19, 1965.
50. Minutes, January 18, 1966.
51. Minutes, October 20, 1970; October 19, 1971.
52. Craig Dykstra and James Hudnut-Beumler, "The National Organizational Structures of Protestant Denominations: An Invitation to Conversation," in Milton J. Coalter, John M. Mulder, and Louis B. Weeks, *The Organizational Revolution: Presbyterians and American Denominationalism* (Louisville, Kentucky: Westminster/John Knox Press, 1992), p. 318.
53. Minutes, March 19, 1963.
54. Minutes, March 18, 1969.
55. Minutes, March 19, 1974.
56. Minutes, March 18, 1975.
57. Minutes, March 19, 1974.
58. Minutes, March 16, 1976.
59. Minutes, March 15, 1977. In fact, by 1982, the classis was seriously asking itself whether it should be in the program business at all. It formed a special committee to consider the matter. They reported that a "strict reading of

the *Book of Church Order* would seem to indicate that program and resource development is not a major concern of classis." The classis adopted the recommendations of its committee that included the conclusion that the classis "do only that level of programming that can be sustained by Classis as a primarily volunteer workforce" and that "the Classis intentionally look to Albany Synod...in the development of more extensive programs and resources." Minutes, October 19, 1982.

60. Minutes, June 18, 1963.
61. Minutes, March 21, 1972.
62. Minutes, March 16, 1971.
63. Minutes, March 17, 1970.
64. Minutes, February 20, 1973.
65. Minutes, March 18, 1975.

Chapter IX

1. Tom Stark, "Supplement to 'A Statement on the Legality of the Ordination and Installation of Mrs. Joyce Stedge...,'" May, 1974, p. 6. Personal files of the author.
2. Schuppert, I, pp. 194-195.
3. Ibid., p. 195.
4. *MGS*, 1958, p. 331.
5. *MGS*, 1973, p. 37.
6. Minutes, June 22, 1976.
7. Minutes, October 21, 1952.
8. Minutes, January 21, 1969.
9. Minutes, June 20, 1978.
10. *MSA*, February 17, 1979, pp. 81-82.
11. *MGS*, 1897, p. 688. Both the synods of New York and New Jersey appealed to the same citation in defense of their action upholding the ordination of women to the office of Minister of the Word.
12. *MGS*, 1957, p. 314.
13. *The Liturgy of the Reformed Church in America together with the Psalter* (New York: The Board of Education, 1968), p. 109.
14. *MGS*, 1979, p. 68.

Index

157